Fastpacking

About the Author

Lily is a writer and a runner based in the Brecon Beacons, Wales. Her childhood was spent in Ireland and the northwest of England and her love of the outdoors grew from studying geology during a natural sciences degree. She started running in her 20s and since then the sport has taken her from pounding the pavements around Birmingham University to running around Manaslu, Nepal, the world's eighth highest mountain. She also enjoys cycle touring and has ridden Land's End to John O'Groats and the loftiest roads of the Himalaya in Ladakh. She still enjoys the buzz of a big-city marathon but is always happiest spending time with friends, beneath open skies and preferably in lumpy places.

Lily is passionate about sharing her love of adventure and the natural world with others. A proportion of author royalties from this book will be donated to nature conservation projects and activity breaks for disadvantaged children.

Inset photo credit: David Palmer
Main photo: Autumn Fastpacking –
Loch Hourn on the west coast of Scotland
(Route 8) (Photo credit: Chris Councell)

Fastpacking

Multi-day running adventures:
tips, stories and route ideas

by Lily Dyu

JUNIPER HOUSE, MURLEY MOSS,
OXENHOLME ROAD, KENDAL, CUMBRIA LA9 7RL
www.cicerone.co.uk

Printed by KHL Printing, Singapore

A catalogue record for this book is available from the British Library.

All photographs are by the author unless otherwise stated.

Route mapping by Lovell Johns

www.lovelljohns.com

© Crown copyright 2018
OS PU100012932.

NASA relief data courtesy of ESRI

Contains OpenStreetMap.org data
© OpenStreetMap contributors, CC-BY-SA.

Acknowledgements

Thanks to Joe at Cicerone for helping to shape this book; to Verity, Andrea and Georgia, my fantastic editors; to the very talented Caroline, for her great design work; and to my writerly friend, Judy Mills, for all her support.

It was a privilege to hear the inspiring stories of all my contributors; this book is dedicated to them, with heartfelt thanks for being so generous with their time and input.

Running has brought so many friends into my life and I'm indebted to all those I've shared the trails with (you know who you are!) Special thanks to Chris for many of the wonderful photographs within these pages and precious memories of shared fastpacking adventures. Without his enthusiasm for crazy capers, this book would not exist.

Updates to this guide

While every effort is made by our authors to ensure the accuracy of guidebooks as they go to print, changes can occur during the lifetime of an edition. Any updates that we know of for this guide will be on the Cicerone website (www.cicerone. co.uk/957/updates), so please check before planning your trip. We also advise that you check information about such things as transport, accommodation and shops locally. Even rights of way can be altered over time.

The non-UK route maps in this guide are derived from publicly available data, databases and crowd-sourced data. As such they have not been through the detailed checking procedures that would generally be applied to a published map from an official mapping agency, although naturally we have reviewed them closely in the light of local knowledge as part of the preparation of this guide.

We are always grateful for information about any discrepancies between a guidebook and the facts on the ground, sent by email to updates@cicerone.co.uk or by post to Cicerone, Juniper House, Murley Moss, Oxenholme Road, Kendal, LA9 7RL.

Register your book: to sign up to receive free updates, special offers and GPX files where available, register your book at www.cicerone.co.uk.

Front cover: Sea views from Mam Meadail, Knoydart, Scotland (Route 8) (Photo credit: Chris Councell)

Contents

⟩ Mountain safety

Every mountain run has its dangers, and those described in this guidebook
are no exception. All who fastpack in the mountains should recognise this and
take responsibility for themselves and their companions along the way. The
author and publisher have made every effort to ensure that the information
contained in this guide was correct when it went to press, but, except for any
liability that cannot be excluded by law, they cannot accept responsibility for
any loss, injury or inconvenience sustained by any person using this book.

To call out the Mountain Rescue, ring 999 (in the UK) or the international
emergency number 112: this will connect you via any available network. Once
connected to the emergency operator, ask for the police.

Symbols used on route maps

～	route
Ⓢ	start point
Ⓕ	finish point
ⓈⒻ	start/finish point
➤	route direction
■	building
▲	youth hostel
⊕	airport
⏶	refuge
	international border
•	summit (UK maps)
▲	peak (non-UK maps)
	glacier
⤫	pass

Himalayan relief
in metres

7600–8000
7200–7600
6800–7200
6400–6800
6000–6400
5600–6000
5200–5600
4800–5200
4400–4800
4000–4400
3600–4000
3200–3600
2800–3200
2400–2800
2000–2400
1600–2000
1200–1600
800–1200
400–800

European relief
in metres

4600–4800
4400–4600
4200–4400
4000–4200
3800–4000
3600–3800
3400–3600
3200–3400
3000–3200
2800–3000
2600–2800
2400–2600
2200–2400
2000–2200
1800–2000
1600–1800
1400–1600
1200–1400
1000–1200
800–1000
600–800
400–600
200–400
0–200

Scales vary widely. Please refer to map for scale.

Relief is relevant to non-UK maps only.

Fastpacking is the art of moving fast and light on multi-day trail-running journeys (Wengen, Switzerland, Route 11) (Photo credit: Chris Councell)

Introduction

Welcome to the world of fastpacking

Fastpacking is a great way for runners to explore and discover new places – Vallone di Vallasco, Italy

Fastpacking is a fast-growing niche in the world of trail running. Put simply, fastpacking is the hybrid of running, hiking and backpacking. It's the art of moving fast and light on multi-day trail running journeys.

To purists, it means being self-sufficient in wild places, experiencing the mountains raw, but there are many styles of trip: from running with a pack between overnight stops, like guesthouses and hostels, to bothying in remote wilderness locations. Hut-to-hut running is increasingly popular in places like the Alps where networks of mountain refuges in spectacular

❯ We were wilderness running. Power hiking. Kind of backpacking, but much faster. More fluid. Neat. Almost surgical. Get in. Get out. I call it fastpacking. ❮

Jim Knight in an article in *UltraRunning* magazine following his 1988 traverse of the Wind River Range, USA. He and his running companion, Bryce Thatcher, completed the 100-mile journey in just 38 hours.

locations provide hot meals and a bed, allowing you to live well and travel light.

Over recent years there has been a boom in trail and ultra-running and stage races. This has evolved into off-shoots such as Fastest Known Times, or FKTs, where runners try to set speed records on established routes, such as Damian Hall completing the UK's 630-mile South West Coast Path in less than 11 days and Kilian Jornet running and climbing over Mont Blanc, starting in Courmayeur and finishing in Chamonix nine hours later.

Multi-day running is not all about times, though. More and more people are pursuing solo running adventures as a way to experience and explore the outdoors. Elise Downing ran the coast of Britain in 301 days, camping and staying with friends, and Anna McNuff covered the length of New Zealand in 148 days, stopping to speak at schools and inspire children to get outside. But you don't need to go far. It could be an out-and-back running trip from your doorstep or following a local long-distance path at a leisurely pace. Fastpacking is for everyone.

Underpinning the activity is the principle of 'fast and light' – taking only what you need to stay safe and happy and nothing more. This allows you to travel further and faster in a day compared to hiking, by running whenever the terrain allows it. You could see it as adventure racing without the race. It's about exploring and enjoying your surroundings at your own pace. It's the excitement and fun of ultras and stage races but without the entry fee and cut-off times. There are no medals, t-shirts

A great way to travel. Ridge running in the Black Mountains of Wales

or personal bests. The reward is the journey itself and the thrill of moving fast and light in the wild. Quite simply, if you love running, fastpacking is a wonderful way to travel and discover new places.

Humans were born to run. Our ancient ancestors were hunter-gatherers, spending days on foot, roaming through the landscape. On a psychological level many of the people who shared their stories for this book spoke of the heightened sense of awareness they experienced in ultra and multi-day running. Such peak experiences and 'flow' may be a huge part of the appeal for those who seek solitude in the natural world through fastpacking.

Perhaps the phenomenal growth of fastpacking is a backlash against our increasingly screen-based, sedentary lives and the constant pressure to record and post every run or ride online. It's a fantastic way to disconnect from our digital lives and reconnect with nature and ourselves. Spending days immersed in the landscape and natural world through fastpacking is, for many runners, a much richer and deeper experience than a trail or ultra race. There is a special satisfaction in making a running journey powered by your own two feet and seeing your surroundings change as you go. And by carrying no more than you need, fastpacking provides a beautiful sense of simplicity and freedom.

You don't need to be an ultra athlete or an extreme adventurer to go fastpacking. It's a lot easier than you'd imagine. And for those who hate planning, there are many companies who will take all of that off your hands, including moving your bags and booking your accommodation, allowing you to just run with a day pack.

This book provides practical tips and advice on organising your own multi-day running trips, including: styles of fastpacking, from supported to unsupported; how to choose a route; where to stay; what to what to take; and eating on multi-day runs.

A question that often comes up when picking a route is, 'How runnable is it?' While a person's ability to run up big climbs and tackle technical terrain is largely a matter of experience, this book also gives overviews and travel tales from 12 tried-and-tested fastpacking routes, including: a wild camping micro-adventure on Dartmoor; running some of the UK's national trails; and a bothy-run in the Highlands. Overseas, there's hut-hopping in the Alps and Dolomites, plus a stage race in Nepal on a tea-house trekking route, along with other fastpacking opportunities in the country.

In addition there are a dozen stories from the world of multi-day running enthusiasts and ultra-distance athletes. In the UK these tales range from bothying in the Black Mountains with Anna McNuff to running from Land's End to John O'Groats with Aly Wren. Iain Harper tackles the Pennine Way in one push, competing in the legendary Spine Race, while Jasmin Paris and her husband, Konrad Rawlik, take a more leisurely approach along the same trails to celebrate her birthday. Further

Fastpacking can take you to remote and inaccessible places – Barrisdale Bay, Scotland (Route 8)

afield, Olly Stephenson takes on the iconic John Muir Trail in the States; Jez Bragg goes hut-to-hut running around Monte Rosa, in Italy and Switzerland; and Anna Frost takes us on a sky-high running journey in Bhutan, the Land of the Thunder Dragon.

By sharing our fastpacking experiences and what we love about multi-day running, we hope that our stories will spark ideas and inspire you to try fastpacking too.

How fit do I need to be?

Fastpacking is for all trail runners. It's not a race and it's up to you how far you go each day. Slowing down is the secret to multi-day running. Compared to a typical run, you can expect to be much slower, mixing running – probably at the pace of a slow training run – with plenty of power-walking. Few people have the fitness to average more than about three miles an hour on hilly or mountainous routes over several days. That's not fast; it's the pace of an average walk.

ᐳ A word about walking

Fastpacking is just like ultra-running in that you will do a lot more walking than you would on a typical long run. This is due to the extra weight on your back and the fact that you're doing it for several days. When fastpacking, most people will usually walk the hills, and run the flats and downhills, unless the terrain is very technical. A leisurely pace also gives you more time to enjoy the views!

How do I train for fastpacking?

If you are already a trail runner, then training for fastpacking has the same principles as preparing for stage races. You need to get your legs and body used to sustained effort over multiple days and to be able to recover quickly. Back-to-back runs – for example, a long run on a Saturday and another on a Sunday – are a key component. The length of these runs would depend on the distances you are aiming to cover in your trip. Although not necessary, you could also squeeze in a brisk run on the Friday so you enter the back-to-back weekend fatigued, to get used to running on tired legs.

To get used to running with a pack you should try a couple of long runs beforehand with a pack slightly lighter than the one you'll be carrying on your trip, perhaps about 5kg.

If you are planning to follow a mountainous or hilly route, you should include hills in your training, to give you leg strength for climbing. Any time spent hiking in the mountains is also great training, because rough trails and big climbs mean you will often be power-walking. Cycling and indoor bike training, such as spinning, are also excellent for building leg strength for hilly terrain.

Strength training of the upper body will prepare your back and shoulder muscles for the effort of running with a pack, while exercises to build core strength will benefit your running posture and speed.

The different styles of fastpacking

Broadly speaking, there are four types of fastpacking – unsupported, where you carry your own food and shelter; running between existing accommodation, such as huts, guesthouses and hostels; self-supported trips, where you might cache food and equipment along the way; and finally, fully supported trips.

Unsupported fastpacking

This is considered by many to be the purest form of the sport because you carry everything you need to be self-sufficient. Your pack will contain a shelter in the form of tent, tarp or bivvy, plus food and sleeping gear. This style is particularly popular in the US where more reliable, dry weather in national parks, such as Yosemite, makes it possible to use a lightweight tent or tarp and carry less clothing, compared to, say, a European or British trip. In the UK, two-day mountain marathon events follow this approach, with runners carrying food and equipment for an overnight camp. Examples of unsupported trips would be two days of running and wild camping in Dartmoor National Park, or taking on the entire Cape Wrath Trail.

Running between existing accommodation

The second variant is running with a small pack between overnight stops, such as mountain huts, guesthouses and hostels. In continental Europe, hut-to-hut running is growing in popularity since there are excellent trail networks coupled with perfectly spaced huts, providing runners with a warm place to sleep and get a hot meal. A lighter pack allows you to enjoy your running more comfortably and to travel further, and by staying in huts you can enjoy the local food and culture, and meet like-minded travellers in the evenings.

Self-supported trips

On these trips, you cache supplies and equipment along the way. An example would be a three-day trip that two runners made across Wales, from Borth on the coast, to Hay-on-Wye on the English border. They doubled up their camping gear by borrowing an extra tent and pair of sleeping bags, and on their drive to the start of the run they dropped off their equipment, along with food for breakfasts and snacks, at two pre-planned campsites en route. They then ran back, sleeping at the campsites and eating in pubs in the evenings. They had to recover their car from the start and collect the camping gear on their drive home, but it was a fun, self-styled adventure.

Supported fastpacking

These are trips where a crew will tend to runners at checkpoints along the route, offering backup in case of an emergency. They are generally the fastest and lightest fastpacking style and also fun and social trips. Every year since 2003, for example, a group of runners from Edinburgh and Aberdeen Hash House Harriers take on an Easter Challenge – a four-day run along a long-distance path or

Mountain huts are usually in spectacular locations.
(Rifugio Morelli – Buzzi, Italy)

Wild camping means you can stop wherever you find your perfect spot (Photo credit: Chris Councell)

a bespoke route – with a driver and minibus. The end point of each day is the next day's starting point. By night, instead of camping, the friends return to a hotel for food, drink and a comfortable bed.

Baggage transfer

Although marketed largely to walkers, it is easy to use baggage transfer services (available on many long-distance routes in the UK) for multi-day runs. For a small cost, your gear will be moved between your overnight stops, allowing you to run with just a day pack carrying essentials. Some companies even deliver bags to campsites. Often hotels can organise this

for you too, using taxis, and there are now companies that offer self-guided trail-running holidays where all of this is taken care of.

Where to stay

On a multi-day route there may be guesthouses, hostels, bunkhouses and hotels to stay at, but when fastpacking there are additional options that allow you to explore wilder, remote or mountainous areas. These are covered below.

Wild camping

For the purist, fastpacking is about being totally self-sufficient through wild camping and carrying all your own gear and food. This has the advantage of allowing you to travel through remote areas and get off the beaten track. Strictly speaking, in the UK this is only officially permitted in Scotland and Dartmoor.

In Scotland you are allowed to camp on most unenclosed land. However, due to overuse, East Loch Lomond is subject to wild camping byelaws which restricts wild camping in the area. Be sure to familiarise yourself with the Scottish Outdoor Access Code (www. outdooraccess-scotland.scot) – basically, campers should follow a policy of 'leave no trace'.

On Dartmoor it is legal to wild camp in some sections of the national park. You can find a map on the national park website (www.dartmoor.gov.uk) which shows the permitted areas. Some sites are used as military firing ranges, so you should always check the firing schedules (www.gov.uk – search 'Dartmoor firing times') as this would override any permission or right to camp.

Elsewhere, in England, Wales and Northern Ireland, wild camping is illegal; the right to stay overnight on open access land is not granted in the Countryside and Rights of Way (CRoW) Act. This means that you cannot wild camp unless you obtain the express permission of the landowner first. In practice, this can often be impractical or impossible to do and wild camping may be tolerated in more remote areas – typically, more than half a day's walk from a campsite or other accommodation – as long as it is done sensitively. The following guidelines should help:

- Arrive late and leave early
- Sleep well above the wall line, away from houses
- Leave no trace of your camp and take out all rubbish
- Don't light fires
- Toilet duties should be performed 30 metres from water and the waste buried
- Pack out all paper and sanitary products
- Be respectful at all times; if asked to move on, do so
- Aim to leave a wild camping spot in better condition than when you found it
- Close gates behind you
- Avoid disturbing wildlife, particularly during the moorland lambing and bird breeding season, from 1 March to 31 July
- Always remember that landowners have the right to move wild campers on.

Bothies

Bothies are free mountain huts in the UK – usually old buildings that are left unlocked for walkers and other outdoors folk to use as an overnight stop. The Mountain Bothies Association maintains, through volunteers, around 100 bothies, mostly in Scotland but with a few in England and Wales, while there are others run by private estates.

Accommodation is basic and camping in a stone tent is a common description for bothying, but they are generally located in wild, remote locations making them a great option for running adventures. When staying in bothies,

Inside Strathchailleach (Sandy's bothy), Sutherland, Scotland

you will often meet new people, which could mean a memorable evening by a fire, sharing stories, food and a hip-flask.

You will, however, still need to carry most, if not all, of the same gear as you would when wild camping. Assume that there will be no facilities – no water, electricity, lights or beds and if there is a fireplace, there probably won't be anything to burn. Also, you will need to carry or find water and there may not be a suitable supply nearby. And bothies generally don't have toilets apart from a spade!

The continued existence of bothies relies on users helping to look after them. The Mountain Bothies Association has developed a Bothy Code which sets out the following guidelines (reproduced with their kind permission):

- The bothies maintained by the MBA are available by courtesy of the owners; please respect this privilege
- Please record your visit in the bothy log-book
- Note that bothies are used entirely at your own risk
- Respect other users
  - Please leave the bothy clean and tidy with dry kindling for the next visitors
  - Make other visitors welcome and be considerate to other users
- Respect the bothy
  - Tell us about any accidental damage. Don't leave graffiti or vandalise the bothy
  - Please take out all rubbish which you can't burn
  - Avoid burying rubbish; this pollutes the environment

- Please don't leave perishable food as this attracts vermin
- Guard against fire risk and ensure the fire is out before you leave
- Make sure the doors and windows are properly closed when you leave
- Respect the surroundings
  - If there is no toilet at the bothy please bury human waste out of sight. Use the spade provided, keep well away from the water supply and never use the vicinity of the bothy as a toilet
  - Never cut live wood or damage estate property. Use fuel sparingly
- Respect agreement with the estate
  - Please observe any restrictions on use of the bothy, for example during stag stalking or at lambing time
  - Please remember bothies are available for short stays only. The owner's permission must be obtained if you intend an extended stay
- Respect the restriction on numbers
  - Because of overcrowding and lack of facilities, large groups (six or more) should not use a bothy

> ## Top tip

Always take a tent, in case the bothy is full, plus a sleeping mat for a more comfortable night's sleep. There may be a sleeping platform, but if it's busy you might have to sleep on a stone floor.

- Bothies are not available for commercial groups.

To find out more, see *The Book of the Bothy* (Cicerone Press) or the Mountain Bothies Association website (www.mountainbothies.org.uk).

Mountain huts

Hut-to-hut running is a fantastic, cost-effective way of fastpacking through the Alps and other European mountain ranges, and it doesn't involve carrying a tent, stove or sleeping bag. Running between mountain huts (also known as refuges, *rifugios*, *Hütten* and *cabanes*), where you can get a bed, hot dinner and breakfast, means you only need to carry essential gear; and a lighter pack means that you can move more quickly and comfortably through mountainous terrain.

High-level mountain huts are an alien concept to many British hikers, and yet there are thousands of them across the continent. They are generally situated at a key pass or high on a mountain, without vehicle access and open from June until October, with some open in the spring ski-touring season. Huts can come in all shapes and sizes, and range from the most basic of bivouac shelters for climbers and mountaineers to larger establishments that almost resemble hotels – imagine a high-altitude hostel with cosy bunks and thick blankets, superb views, hearty food, and a common room filled with outdoorsy types from all over the world. Huts let you travel light and live well, costing typically €50 a night for half-board, for a bed in

Hut-hopping is great way to travel. Refuge de la Croix de Bonhomme on the Tour du Mont Blanc, France (Route 9)

a dormitory or twin room. Although a mattress and bedding are provided, you must also bring and use your own sheet sleeping bag.

Huts are a tourism industry in themselves. In an Italian *rifugio*, you might enjoy multi-course meals, a bar, proper Italian coffee, showers and drying facilities. Some even have hot tubs outside! Meanwhile, Norway's huts are often unstaffed and work on a basis of co-operation and trust. You are relied on to make a payment for a stay and food taken from their stores, and to leave things the way you found them. Well equipped, cosy, comfortable and warm, with plenty of firewood, these make a welcoming stay after a day on the trails.

Guidebooks are usually the best source of information on the existence and location of huts, but many refuges now have their own websites giving details of accommodation, facilities and contact details so that you can book ahead. Appendix A includes the websites of the main European Alpine Clubs, where you will also find hut information.

The Mountain Hut Book (Cicerone Press) is an excellent introduction to mountain huts and refuges for walkers and trekkers. It explores the mountain hut experience, from how huts have developed to modern-day hut etiquette, and also includes profiles of the author's favourite refuges and recommended hut-to-hut routes in the Alps and Pyrenees.

› Top tips

- Membership of the UK branch of the Austrian Alpine Club – www.aacuk.org.uk – is worth considering as this includes rescue insurance and hut discounts.

- Members of the British Mountaineering Council – www.thebmc.co.uk – can buy a Reciprocal Rights Card which gives discounted rates in huts, including those owned by the Alpine Clubs of France, Switzerland, Germany, Holland, South Tyrol, Austria and Spain.

- Membership of the Alpine Club – www.alpine-club.org.uk – also provides some hut discounts.

- Always check a hut is open when you are visiting. Have an idea of where you will stay and book ahead in high season, when huts will often be busy with both walkers and locals using them for weekend activities. Bed spaces and meals at huts can usually be booked via email and phone.

- September is often a great time for Alpine fastpacking. The weather is usually good and, since it's out of season, the huts usually aren't as busy.

Where should I go fastpacking?

As important as it is to pack light, choosing your route is perhaps key to your enjoyment – whether you design your own or follow an existing one. Fastpacking is about running to a place you can't get to in just a day and there are many ways of doing this, from a short, out-and-back trip with an overnight stay, to doing a national trail over several days, to planning your own

journey lasting weeks. Some adventurers have even run around the world.

Fastpacking routes fall into two categories: the 'loop', which starts and ends at the same place; and the 'through route', which is linear in nature and may require the additional logistics of returning to the start.

For time reasons, loops are often preferred by fastpackers, especially on shorter trips. These make great weekend micro-adventures, such as a two-day run on the Gower Peninsula, stopping at a bunkhouse – but they could be longer journeys, as in a full five-day circuit of Mont Blanc.

Through routes are great for longer trips, giving the satisfaction of making a point-to-point journey under your own steam and seeing your surroundings constantly change. However, you will need to factor in the logistics of

A cloud inversion in the Italian Alps on the Grand Traversata delle Alpi (Photo credit: Chris Councell)

Breathtaking Glen Affric on a multi-day run across Scotland

travelling back to the start or perhaps to a different location. Trips you could try include taking a train out to a start point and running home over two or three days, or perhaps following an existing long-distance route such as a national trail.

Designing your own route

Researching and planning your own route allows you to take in the landmarks you want to see, trails you want to run or perhaps hills you want to climb.

While training for the Marathon des Sables, for example, two friends ran 25 miles of the Wye Valley Walk, from Hay-on-Wye to Hereford, with an overnight stop at a guesthouse, and then back via the same route the next day.

Another group of fell runners head up to Scotland each year with lightweight mountain marathon gear so they can run and walk their own routes over a long weekend. One of their most memorable journeys was a three-day, two-night trip, parking at Muir of Ord and getting the train across to Attadale on the west coast, then running back and wild camping along the way, far from roads and staying high on the hills. You can simply pick a place you've always wanted to visit and design a trip around it.

Long-distance walking routes

Choosing established routes, whether in the UK, Europe or further afield, generally means that there will be good transport connections, accommodation and services en route, making organisation and logistics much easier. There are often luggage-moving services available too. From a planning perspective, guidebooks and maps will be readily available, as well as online resources.

The UK has many well-established national trails and fantastic land access for walkers who enjoy the right to roam in much of the countryside and open spaces. You can camp or stay at hostels, bothies, hotels, bunkhouses and guesthouses. On European walking routes you will usually find fantastic networks of mountain huts and budget walkers' accommodation, making them an excellent choice for fastpacking.

Another great resource is the Long Distance Walkers Association. Their website gives information on over 1500 long-distance routes in the UK, with links to books, maps and accommodation. For a small annual fee, as a member, you also get access to events and newsletters. See www.ldwa.org.uk

Ultra-marathon race routes

The routes of ultra-marathon races make a great choice for fastpacking

Approaching Hay-on-Wye at the end
of a three-day run across Wales
(Photo credit: Chris Councell)

trips and their route maps and GPX files are usually available on event organiser websites. Often competitors will use fastpacking as a way of training and doing a route 'recce'. An advantage of these is that the race route is likely to be very runnable – although there won't necessarily be much accommodation available along the way.

> ## Top tip

Whether designing your own route or following an existing trail, choose a schedule that leaves room for adventure and taking in the views. It's not a race!

Distance

What is the total distance of this route? What daily mileage is realistic and achievable? How long do you want to be out for each day? Some people like to start early and finish in the early afternoon, giving them plenty of time to refuel, recover and perhaps wash their gear. You might simply choose to run a standard walking stage each day, giving you more time to stop at cafés, enjoy the views and explore in comparison to walking; while more experienced runners may opt for full 12-hour days in the mountains. It's a personal

The UK has many national trails that are perfect for fastpacking trips

choice, to be decided by factoring in all information about the route.

Height gain and loss

What is the total daily ascent and descent? This is critical to how far you can cover each day. In fastpacking you will be generally walking the climbs and running the descents and flats and this is how you gain time compared to walking, thus allowing you to go further. But if your route is exceptionally hilly, with lots of steep climbs, technical descents and little flat, you may find that it's impossible to run and you will actually be no quicker than a hiker.

Difficulty of the terrain

This is crucial to your safety and also how far you can realistically travel in a day. How technical is the terrain? Will

you be on smooth, easy, well-made trails that are easy to run on? Will rocky, rough ground slow you down on the flat? Does a steep, technical descent mean you won't be able to run downhill? Will there be river crossings that slow you down or require a lengthy diversion? Again, very technical terrain means that you may not be able to do much running.

Some routes include scrambling and exposure, which you may not be happy doing, especially in running shoes and certainly not without previous experience. On many Alpine routes there may be trails with via ferrata, or aided and assisted sections using ropes and ladders. In fastpacking you won't be in the same gear as a hiker and these could be treacherous in running shoes and without the right equipment. Read

› Top tips

- Research and plan your route thoroughly and understand its technical difficulty.

- If considering a mountainous route, read a guidebook beforehand, using a highlighter to pick out technical sections. Consider these carefully before making a final route choice. Partway through a multi-day mountain trip is too late to discover that there are sections of route that you are not equipped for or sufficiently experienced to undertake.

- Be flexible. There is no shame in missing out sections and using public transport to connect up more runnable, scenic and interesting sections.

- Identify escape points where you can leave a route if necessary.

- Plan for recoverable daily efforts. On any multi-day trip, aim to be just as strong on the last as you were on the first day.

all available information about a route carefully and decide if it's within your capability.

Navigation

Although spending time navigating may slow your running pace, it's easy to overshoot and miss a turn when running, so it's worth stopping regularly to check your location. Always carry a map and compass and know how to use them. A good navigator will always have these to hand, rather than in their pack. Ensure you are competent in navigating in poor conditions.

Always know where you are on the map when following a route. It's easy to forget to check this while you're caught up in the flow of running, but you don't want to suddenly reach a path junction and wonder where you are. While you're running it can be difficult to keep track of your position and this will mean

Always factor in navigation when estimating your running pace

Always check what terrain to expect and whether it's within your capability (Passo di Ciotto Mieu, Italian Alps)

you need to re-find your location each time you look at the map. To get around this, a good technique to use is 'thumbing the map'. This simply means always having your thumb next to your current position on the map and moving it along the route, as you compare map features to the observed terrain, while you run.

Obviously, night navigation experience is a bonus if you're caught late on the trails due to unforeseen circumstances. In these situations, you should also act with risk aversion in mind and try to find the easiest route to navigate – for example by switching to quiet

> ## Mobile phones and GPS devices

There are, on the market, countless GPS devices, including GPS watches that can navigate for you. There are also many useful GPS apps available for smartphones – if you're buying one, choose a product that lets you download maps so you can view them offline. These apps will locate your position on a map even if you have no mobile coverage; this can be useful for cross-checking your location. A very popular GPS app is Viewranger – www.viewranger.com – which runs on both iOS and Android devices and can be downloaded from the Apple App Store or Google Play.

roads rather than mountain paths to get to your destination.

Don't rely solely on electronic equipment for navigation as it can fail, or you may find you are unable to charge your device on your trip. A good rule is to treat a smartphone as an emergency device. Be aware that batteries run down more quickly in the cold. Always use a waterproof cover. Keep your device safe in a pocket in a waterproof bag, in airplane mode, with no apps running in the background to conserve battery life. Rely on your own navigation skills.

Safety

The most important thing a runner will take on a fastpacking trip is their outdoor know-how. Mountain weather can change very quickly; you need to have the skills to take care of yourself and others before you head into the mountains and remote places. These include navigation, first aid, what to do in an emergency, river crossings, and an understanding of mountain weather, hypothermia and the effects of heat.

If you are not skilled enough to hike a route, then never fastpack it, since running increases your risk of an

> ### Top tips

- Start early each day. This provides contingency in case something unexpected happens, like getting lost or encountering poor weather.
- Make sure you know what weather conditions are likely. Are afternoon thunderstorms common in the region you're planning to fastpack in? Will there be snow and ice on a high pass? Ensure you know how to deal with these situations.
- Build your experience by trying fastpacking on shorter trips before attempting long-distance routes. Learn as you go and build skills and confidence.
- Fastpacking means going fast and light, but without

compromising safety. **Never** omit essential clothes and equipment for the conditions, no matter how light you'd like your pack to be.
- Take a charged phone and avoid using it apart from in emergencies.
- Ideally, go fastpacking in company.
- Leave your itinerary with someone at home. Make sure someone knows where you are going to be and when you should be expected to return, especially if you are travelling solo.
- Plan for emergencies and have exit points planned along your route so that, if necessary, you can get out safely.

accident. Fastpacking presents unique challenges compared to hiking, since you will be in different footwear and probably carrying less equipment and clothing.

That said, some people have argued that going lighter and faster allows you to remove yourself from risks, like poor mountain weather, more quickly. This clearly depends on your experience and you should never compromise on safety when making gear choices. It's a classic balance of your experience, the likely conditions, terrain and carrying the necessary gear to be safe.

How to get started

It's a good idea to start with a simple overnight trip, for example running a circuit close to home that includes an overnight stay, or an out-and-back route. You could take the train somewhere and then run back to your start. Short trips allow you to build up experience of back-to-back running days while carrying a pack.

The UK's national trails are a great way to try fastpacking and generally these aren't technically difficult or very mountainous. You could opt to use a baggage service to move your gear and this would let you get used to running longer distances over consecutive days, before carrying the weight of a heavier pack.

What to take

Obviously, what you carry will depend on the type of trip you're doing, whether you're camping or running between accommodation, but the key principle in fastpacking is to travel as light as possible. A heavy pack will make it both uncomfortable and impossible to run. But you should never compromise on safety – you need the right gear to take care of yourself and to be prepared for the likely conditions. Carry exactly what you need to be safe and happy, and nothing more. A full suggested kit list is provided in Appendix B.

The contents of my rucksack for two weeks in the Italian Alps

Backpacks

Your pack is your most important piece of kit and needs to be comfortable, fit well and hold all your gear. There is an excellent range available due to the growth in ultra-running, so it's just a matter of finding one that rides well on your body and meets your needs. Here are some factors to consider when choosing:

- Volume – when wild camping you will need 25–30 litres; for an Alpine hut-to-hut trip, 15–25 litres is probably sufficient; and for a UK national trail using existing accommodation, 10–15 litres is plenty
- Comfort – choose a pack with a soft back-pad that moulds to the shape of your back
- Stability – comfortable and stabilising straps around the shoulders and across the sternum are crucial. You should be able to pull the waist belt, shoulder straps and chest strap tightly to eliminate as much movement of the pack as possible

- Rubbing – when running, there should be very little motion of the pack against your back, both horizontally and vertically. If your pack moves, it will make it hard to run and lead to painful pack-rub
- Pockets on the waistband or straps are useful for quick access to essential items such as head torch, snacks, map and compass, and camera. With some packs, you can also buy map pouches that attach to the front of the pack
- Camera access – invest in a specialist pouch that can be attached to your chest straps at the front, or waist belt, allowing easy access. If your camera is in your main pack, you are unlikely to use it.

Sleeping bags

Your sleeping bag needs to pack down small without compromising on warmth. Much of your recovery happens when you are sleeping, so being comfortable at night is important. Down sleeping bags are lighter and

The weight of your pack is the most crucial factor for enjoyable and successful fastpacking

pack down smaller than their synthetic counterparts; however, a good ultra-light down sleeping bag is not cheap. If your bag gets wet then synthetic will be warmer than down because feathers clump together.

Your sleeping bag will be a personal choice and what you take will depend on the expected conditions. You can also buy fleece liners or consider a silk liner for additional insulation. Your spare clothes packed into a stuff sack will make for a comfy pillow.

› Top tips

- Before buying a pack, try running with it, loaded with some gear.

- Women may find that many unisex packs don't fit well, even with straps pulled tightly. In recent years, however, designers are paying attention to the need for a good fit on different body sizes, so the range has improved with women-specific packs available. Make sure you test the pack.

- Keep your clothes, sleeping bag, and any electronic equipment dry by putting them in ultra-light waterproof stuff sacks or plastic bags. Freezer or Ziploc bags are ideal. In addition to this, a waterproof cover for your pack will prevent it becoming heavy and sodden in rain. Also watch out for sweat soaking into your pack from your back.

Sleeping mat

A sleeping mat is worth the extra weight for the added comfort and insulation from the ground. In bothies these will provide cushioning from the sleeping platform or stone floor.

Foam mats are cheap, light, comfortable and good at insulating against the cold but are cumbersome to carry. Self-inflating mats tend to be fairly light (but often a little heavier than foam), comfortable and pack down small, but are usually much more expensive. There are some very lightweight mats on the market that you can inflate with your breath or even using a 'pump sack', which is a stuff sack that doubles as a pump. Some mats are now designed with gaps and holes to reduce weight. As with sleeping bags, there are many options available.

Many running packs, designed for mountain marathons, have a removable back pad that you can use as a sleeping mat beneath your upper back and shoulders. Some people might make do with this, cushioning the rest of their body with their empty pack. If you want to try this, experiment with a one-night trip first.

Shelters – tent, tarp or bivvy?

When should you take a tent versus a tarp? Your choice of shelter depends on the weather and how exposed you are prepared to be. If you are likely to encounter heavy rain or insects, a tent will provide more space, comfort and protection. If it's going to be dry, you might be happy with a lightweight tarp – a rectangle of nylon or plastic that you set up as a shelter in whatever way best suits your needs. A tarp means sleeping without any walls, groundsheet or insect netting but you will be

Camping beneath a tarp while fastpacking on the John Muir Trail, Sierra Nevada, United States (Photo credit: Olly Stephenson)

more connected with nature, as you are essentially sleeping outdoors.

There are also tarp tents, a lightweight hybrid of the two, but as with other outdoor gear there's a direct correlation between the cost of gear and how much it weighs. Super-lightweight tents and tarp tents that you may like to use on a fastpacking trip aren't cheap.

Finally, a bivvy bag or even just sleeping bag without a shelter are both options if the weather is going to be good. Read Ronald Turnbull's classic *Book of the Bivvy* (Cicerone Press) for advice and amusing accounts of his bivvying adventures.

Tents

Most one or two-person tents weigh around 2kg but advances in materials have seen weights come tumbling down to nearer 1kg or less, although lighter tents will be more expensive. A new tent may be unsealed, seam-sealed or fully waterproof with factory-taped seams. Water can potentially find its way into any tent through needle holes in the seams or through an accidental pinhole or tear, so it's worth checking the manufacturer's recommendations for seam-sealing your shelter if this hasn't already been done. This is usually straightforward and simply means applying a sealant product (available from outdoor stores or online) to all the tent seams. Most commercially available tents have been factory seam-sealed and some will need to be re-sealed every few years, to keep your shelter in good condition.

› Top tip

When fastpacking with a second person, split the tent and camping equipment between you.

Tarp tents

A tarp tent is a tent with wall, insect netting and groundsheet but it is significantly lighter than a regular tent because it combines the rain fly-sheet and inner tent into a single wall instead of two layers. Besides its weight, another advantage is that it sets up very quickly in the rain because the entire tent pitches as a complete unit. In addition, some tarp tents can be pitched using hiking poles instead of having to carry additional tent-poles, saving further weight, and some can be turned fully into a traditional tarp, without a groundsheet, in good weather.

Tarps

If you go for a tarp, be sure to try it out before starting your trip, to practise pitching it as a shelter – perhaps even using your running poles. Think about whether you want a groundsheet and/or bivvy bag to complement it. A groundsheet is good if you're fastpacking in climates where the ground is perpetually damp or if wet weather is expected. Some people even forgo this and sleep on their waterproof gear to save extra weight. Heavy dew can soak a sleeping bag, so some people choose to pair a tarp with a lightweight bivvy bag. Additionally, if bugs and insects are likely to be an issue, you could consider buying a lightweight mesh shelter for extra protection.

Bivvy bags

Bivvy bags are another lightweight option and provide a fully waterproof tube into which you put your sleeping bag. Some also provide a bug screen that goes over your face. You could use this set-up in lieu of all other shelters, but always look for a bivvy bag with breathable fabric, otherwise you may have an issue with moisture from inside the bivvy soaking your sleeping bag.

Head torch

The head torch you should take on a fastpacking trip will depend on how you plan to use it. If you will be doing any night running and hiking, you'll need something with a powerful output for route-finding and good vision on the trail. Something less powerful and

lighter may be sufficient if you are just using it at camp or at your accommodation. Always consider carrying spare batteries.

> ### Top tip
>
> Always carry a head torch on a fastpacking trip, in case you make slower progress than planned and accidentally end up on a trail in the dark or fading light.

Running poles

In mountainous terrain, running poles help enormously with the climbing and technical descents. They reduce effort and impact and help when you're getting tired. They are also useful for crossing rivers and for testing marshy ground, to see how deep bogs are. There are lightweight poles on the

Running poles are invaluable in mountainous terrain. (Above Rifugio Genova, Italian Alps)

market designed specifically for runners, which can be folded down easily.

Clothing

Your clothes will be a significant weight in your pack, and the goal here is to pack minimally while ensuring you have everything you need for the expected conditions. It's a classic balancing act that requires you to question whether every item has a place on your trip.

While more experienced ultra-runners might manage a hut-to-hut trip carrying only the compulsory kit for the Ultra-Trail du Mont Blanc (UTMB) race, others might want more gear – but always remember that pack weight will significantly affect your enjoyment of the trip.

General advice

- Always take waterproof trousers and jacket, with fully taped seams, even if the forecast looks benign. Conditions can change unexpectedly and hypothermia is potentially fatal. Even if it doesn't rain, these provide extra insulation and a windproof layer.
- Waterproofs should be fully breathable because you will be sweating from running. They will also be subject to increased rubbing from your pack due to your running movement, so it helps to re-proof these regularly.
- Merino wool tops are brilliant for fastpacking. They do not smell even after being worn for days, which means that you can usually manage a trip with one or two tops that won't need hand-washing. They come in different thicknesses and you can get lightweight t-shirts, vests or thicker base layers. You can also get merino underwear and leggings.
- Avoid thick seams on tops because these will rub between your pack and skin. Where seams are unavoidable, choose flat-locked seams.
- Wear a top that will cover the entire surface area of your pack. Fastpacking in a sports bra or a vest will rub your skin where the pack is in contact with it.
- Women should look for seamless sports bras, with close-fitting and flat straps.
- Consider cutting out labels to avoid chafing.
- Always consider multi-use for different items of gear. A pair of running tights will be travel-wear, evening-wear or running-wear when it's cold or wet. A fleece top for the evening will be an extra running layer if it gets cold. A Buff could be a beanie, headband, travel towel or wrist sweat-band.
- Whatever you wear on your legs, whether shorts, capri or tights, it is critical that these do not chafe.
- Carry detergent so you can hand-wash shorts and underwear. This helps to prevent chafing. Technical fabrics will usually dry out overnight. You can also use cord to attach these to your pack to dry during the day.
- Do not try anything new. Stick to tried and trusted gear that you are happy with on long runs carrying a pack.

Make sure you're prepared for quickly changing weather (Reichenbach stream, Switzerland, Route 11) (Photo credit: Chris Councell)

- Pack for your destination and the worst conditions you might encounter. If it's 30 degrees outside a city hotel room when you're packing, don't forget that in an Alpine hut at 3000m you may see snow even in summer.
- Travel wearing your spare running gear and running shoes. Don't carry around spare clothes for your flight or return journey – this is dead weight. Accept that you will look like a gnarly adventurer from when you leave your front door. This also makes life simple since you have no clothing choices to make!
- For overseas trips, if starting and returning to the same place, you can leave a bag of gear at a hotel, airport or train station for your return journey or the rest of your trip.

Footwear

As fastpacking can be done in any environment, footwear should be chosen based on the conditions you will encounter and the distance you plan to travel. Shoes are a highly personal choice, but here is some general advice:

- For long distances over multiple days, trail-running shoes with plenty of cushioning and protection are ideal. Protection around the foot and toe box is needed to protect your feet on rocky trails
- Cushioning is crucial. Without enough cushioning, days of running on hard trails can bruise the soles of your feet and this can end your trip. Stones and rocks jab up into the soles of your shoes more when you are running with a pack. Inserting Sorbathane insoles into your shoes is good for extra cushioning
- On rocky, wet trails, or grass and mud, you will want a shoe with a good traction for that terrain. Trusting the grip on your shoes is crucial to safety and can also make the difference between loving and loathing your trip
- Test shoes in the terrain that you are likely encounter, especially if you are heading into mountains. Wearing trail-running shoes on mountain footpaths is very different to walking boots, which usually have better grip on wet rock, plus ankle support

› Top tip

If you don't have a second pair of shoes for the evening you can keep your socks dry in damp shoes by wearing plastic bags on your feet – a favourite tip of mountain marathon competitors.

- A luxury item is flip-flops or lightweight canvas shoes. These are not essential but it's nice to get out of running shoes at the end of the day. Many mountain huts provide Croc-type plastic shoes.

Running gaiters
Running gaiters are handy for keeping stones and debris out of your shoes. They may also help to keep your feet and socks dry.

Micro-spikes
These are worth considering if you think you may encounter any late snow on Alpine routes in the summer. However, they are not adequate for glacier crossings, which would be a whole book chapter on their own.

Waterproof socks
Gore-Tex waterproof socks are great for keeping your feet warmer and drier for longer than ordinary socks, but they're not cheap. If you only have damp running shoes to wear in the evenings, these will help keep your feet dry. They won't keep all water out – for example if you ford a stream where the water is above the sockline – and they also take longer to dry out after washing than ordinary socks.

Food
While fastpacking, even if you're not covering a marathon distance each day, your daily energy requirements may be comparable to those for a marathon – or even greater – due to the demands of carrying a pack and the hilly or mountainous terrain. Unlike in a marathon, your body will not have the benefits of rest and recovery, since you will be making these demands over sustained multiple days.

Eating and nutrition will therefore play an important role in your trip. Fastpacking gives you licence to eat a lot! It's important to eat frequently while you're moving and to adequately refuel in the evenings. Runners will have their own preferences for food and an eating schedule, but the main advice here is to remember your energy requirements will be high and to ensure that you stay fuelled and hydrated throughout.

Food on unsupported trips
Fastpackers who wild camp fall into two categories when it comes to food: cold or hot. Some people carry only food they can eat cold, so they can avoid taking a stove and fuel. For others, a hot drink and meal at the end of the day is worth the extra weight, especially if it's been wet and cold.

> ## Top tip
>
> Take care with foot placement while fastpacking. On a trip where you're jogging and hiking all day with weight on your back, rocks and stones jabbing into your feet will start to hurt a lot. Watch the ground and try to land on flat surfaces when you can.

As a vegetarian, this was not one of my best mountain hut dinners! (Photo credit: Chris Councell)

Cooking and eating utensils

Choose a camping stove that is small and lightweight and will heat up water quickly. A collapsible cup, which you can use to eat hot food, and a Spork are good choices to keep weight down.

Food on non-camping trips

If you aren't camping, and are running between accommodation, then you have options. In the evenings you can dine in, eat out or perhaps self-cater, depending on your lodgings and access to shops. During the day you can carry a packed lunch and your own snacks; buy your food en route; or stop for lunch at a pub, café or mountain hut.

Runners will know from experience what is likely to suit them best. Some people carry gels and bars while others find these get sickly and prefer 'real' food. In the Alps, some people might manage by grazing as they run, while others might stop for a proper meal in a refuge, where they can also replenish their snacks. If you've become wet and cold, the benefits of a hot meal and drink can't be overstated.

Guesthouses and mountain huts can often provide a packed lunch. Check your route to see if you pass towns and villages where you can buy food, so that you don't need to carry much. Always carry at least 400 calories of spare food or gels in case of emergencies.

Each runner will have their own preferences for camping food and eating while moving, so no advice is included here on specific products; however, for a trip over multiple days, weight will be key. Some people take a scientific approach to researching and choosing the most calorie-dense foods and matching the quantities to their daily energy requirements.

> ### ⟩ Top tip
>
> If you are headed into colder conditions, take an extra 500 calories per day as your energy needs will be higher, in order to maintain your body temperature.

Water

Staying hydrated while fastpacking is critical, given the high levels of exertion from running long distances with a pack. You should drink plenty of water

Preparing a fastpacking dinner in a bothy (Photo credit: Tori James)

and have your water bottles or bladder drinking tube easily accessible at the front of your pack. As well as drinking on the trail, it is also crucial to rehydrate well in the mornings and evenings during your trip. This is to avoid the risk of severe dehydration which is a possible cumulative effect of multiple back-to-back days of being dehydrated.

As weight is key, you should plan carefully how much water to carry and where you can fill up en route. It is therefore critical, when planning, to understand where your water sources are going to be, whether that's a shop, a stream or a mountain hut that you'll be passing.

If you're wild camping you should aim to camp near a river or stream. This will mean studying your map and route carefully so that you know where you'll be able to get water. Most bothies are near a water source and this is generally shown on the MBA website

It's worth investing in a lightweight, collapsible water carrier for these trips.

While some people drink from rivers and streams without treating the water first, it is best to always err on the side of caution. Nasty water-borne diseases are easy to pick up.

The simplest way to purify water is by boiling it on your camping stove. If you want to save fuel, you can buy chemicals or purification tablets to treat water. If you are squeamish about muddy-looking water, you can filter larger particles out through a Buff first. Other options are lightweight filters, ultra-violet filters and even a straw with a filter on it which lets you drink straight from the water source.

Whichever method you use, always try to take water from a fast-flowing stream, as opposed to standing water, and preferably above the tree line. Avoid areas where there are cattle, sheep or other livestock as there could be a dead animal upstream, or water-borne bacteria from livestock.

Tips for staying happy and healthy

- Women should be aware that the menstrual cycle can be affected by physical, physiological and emotional stress, all of which can occur at high altitude. Periods can be missed altogether, or become heavier, longer, shorter or irregular. Jet lag, physical exertion, cold

Chilling your legs in icy water can help to reduce muscle soreness and weight loss can also alter the pattern. Be aware of this particularly if you are fastpacking at high altitude. Pack sanitary items even if you aren't expecting your period during your trip.

- Carry antibacterial gel and practise good hand-hygiene.
- Use tape to cover areas on the soles and heels of your feet that you know are prone to becoming hotspots.
- Carry toilet paper in case you get caught out. Bury toilet waste and either burn or carry out toilet paper and sanitary items.
- Use Vaseline to prevent chafing. Sustained, multiple days of running can result in chafing even for runners who've run countless marathons with no previous issues. This can ruin your time outdoors.

- Sunglasses are a must for high-altitude routes and also protect your eyes from the glare from rock and snow.
- At the end of the day, immersing your legs in cold water, whether in a bath, shower or river, followed by hot water where possible, is great for preventing muscle soreness.
- Be prepared to make emergency repairs to kit, clothes and packs, and carry spare shoe laces.
- Carry and use a chap stick for the harsh conditions of sun, wind and altitude.
- Take care of issues early – as soon as they arise – to prevent them spoiling your trip. Don't wait until a hotspot on your foot becomes a blister, or for your back to be rubbed raw from your pack.

Inspiration

Fastpacking is about enjoying your
surroundings at your own pace
(Grand Col Ferret, Tour du Mont Blanc, Route 9)

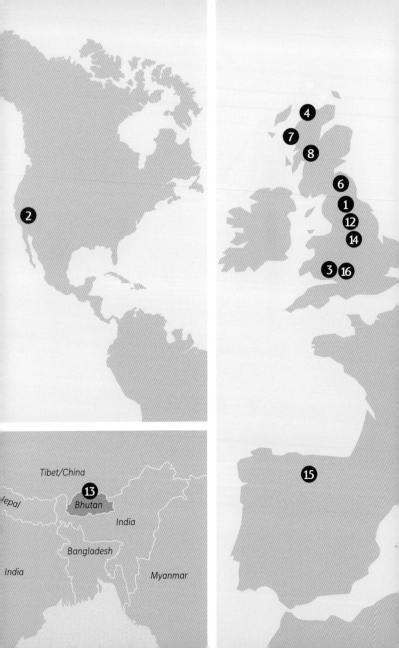

Ready to go at Kirk Yetholm (Photo credit: Jasmin Paris and Konrad Rawlik collection)

A PENNINE PASSAGE

A birthday run along the backbone of England with Jasmin Paris and Konrad Rawlik

Keld appeared to be abandoned for winter. This was the intersection of the Coast-to-Coast and Pennine Way, where the guidebook had painted a picture of a bustling village – but this was a ghost town. They were starting to feel cold, walking beneath moonlight through dark, silent lanes. Turning a corner, they saw a house with lights on. Konrad knocked on the door and explained to the owner that they needed somewhere to stay. She invited the pair in and made calls to friends, further and further away before a guesthouse was eventually found.

It was November 2015 and Jasmin Paris and her husband, Konrad Rawlik, were at the end of their fourth day of running the Pennine Way. Both are well known for their running achievements: Jasmin has been national fell running champion; she's the fastest woman over the Bob Graham and Paddy Buckley rounds and holds the overall record for the Charlie Ramsay – all achieved in an astonishing six months in 2016. Konrad has won the Fellsman race and also placed third in the Dragon's Back. The couple have twice raced the multi-day Transalpine together.

For both, this was simply to be a week's holiday to celebrate Jasmin's birthday, following the route that starts at Kirk Yetholm, close to their home in Scotland, and finishes at Edale near her parents' place in Derbyshire. 'When she first suggested it,' laughs Konrad, 'I said that taking the TransPennine Express to her parents for her birthday was a great idea!'

That evening they ran two extra miles from Keld to their eventual bed for the night. 'It was a really nice family-run B&B,' recalls Jasmin. 'They weren't expecting anyone and their boiler was being repaired, so they put the kettle on and gave us bowls of water to wash our muddy legs. We'd expected to eat in the pub so we asked if we could have our cooked breakfast for tea instead. We had a fry-up in the evening and cereal and toast the next morning!'

Their journey so far had been a joy, taking them over the Cheviot hills floating on a sea of cloud, where they had met a herd of wild goats – a highlight for Konrad as a fan of those much-maligned creatures, and for Jasmin a trigger for an unexpected craving for goat's cheese.

'We loved the first day,' says Konrad. 'The Cheviots were the wildest section, with the most fell running. On the second day Hadrian's Wall was really special – running alongside it towards an amazing sunset. Everything was orange and pink. There was a lovely autumn light. It was spectacular.'

On Cross Fell, the highest point of the route, they were chased along a ridge by wind, rain and hail before dropping to Dufton. This was followed by a perfect day above the rift of High Cup Nick and passing High Force.

'Each day had its own special moment,' says Konrad, 'like getting to the Tan Hill Inn, having a hot chocolate and then running in the dark down to Keld. The sky was clear and all the stars were out. It was beautiful.'

Knowing few people would be walking the route at that time of year, they had decided against pre-booking accommodation. 'Planning a 270-odd-mile run in Britain during November is no easy task,' Konrad jokes, 'so I decided to largely avoid any planning!'

Typical terrain on the northern sections of the Pennine Way
(Photo credit: Jasmin Paris and Konrad Rawlik collection)

Finding rooms wasn't to be easy, though. On their second night they ran an extra three miles, from Greenhead to Gilsland, for somewhere to stay, and the following night they trudged through Dufton until they stumbled across a farmhouse B&B on the outskirts of the village. Here, however, the local pub wasn't serving meals and Jasmin's pleas to buy some bread and cheese didn't yield any success. Thankfully, their B&B host came to the rescue, with the drive to collect her daughter from bad-minton being diverted to the nearest fish and chip shop.

Jasmin and Konrad weren't carrying much food apart from some flapjack, along with essentials, in their 15-litre packs. Instead of taking extra shoes they'd opted for the mountain marathon trick of plastic bags on their feet to keep their socks dry in the evening. Each had only one set of running gear.

'Go light,' is Jasmin's advice to anyone contemplating fastpacking. 'You really don't need much. It was enjoyable because we had such light packs. If you carry too much, it's not much fun because you have to walk. All our evening gear was hill clothes you could put on in an emergency.'

Day five was Jasmin's birthday, so to avoid the hassle of previous days they phoned ahead to book a room for the night. Sunshine and iconic terrain, familiar from the Fellsman and Three Peaks races, led them to Horton-in-Ribblesdale, their agreed second tea-stop of the day. Regular tea breaks were a crucial ingredient of the holiday.

Spectacular autumn sunset at Hadrian's wall on day two
(Photo credit: Jasmin Paris and Konrad Rawlik collection)

High Force in Teesdale on day four, one of many sights along the way (Photo credit: Jasmin Paris and Konrad Rawlik collection)

'We both love a cuppa,' says Jasmin, 'but Konrad lives for cake. The more tea-stops we could have, the better! Even when we raced the Transalpine, that was our ethos. Just having fun together. We were running hard, but every day we'd finished by mid-day so we still went for ice cream sundaes and went swimming. Other competitors were more serious – some would only have gels – but we'd try the local food in the aid stations. So although we weren't exactly sightseeing, it was still a very enjoyable week away.'

Disappointingly, the café in Horton-in-Ribblesdale was shut, so bowls of soup from the pub fuelled them over Pen-y-Ghent. From here they crossed limestone pavement in the gathering dusk before descending past the cove to the twinkling lights of Malham, where a three-course dinner and bottle of wine awaited them.

'It was an award-winning B&B,' recalls Jasmin. 'The morning after my birthday, we ate so much breakfast it was bouncing around in our stomachs. Luckily it was a downhill section, so we could just roll along!'

Achilles pain then saw Jasmin experimenting with barefoot running through farm-land to the foot of Haworth Moor before reverting to shoes for the climb, post-tea-stop, over Stoodley Pike and then the descent to Mankinholes. Here, they were staying at the youth hostel where a sign warned about the pub: 'Don't go if you want good service!'

– but in fact they enjoyed a surprisingly tasty dinner there. The hostel itself wasn't offering meals, but the warden sold them tins of Tesco Value custard and rice pudding for breakfast. The following day would be their last, with 43 miles to cover.

By mid-morning the next day the two runners, in shorts and brightly coloured waterproofs, were sitting on plastic chairs by a catering van, next to the M62. Sheltering from drizzle and the roar of traffic, they drank tea and ate flapjack whilst being stared at by the lorry drivers on neighbouring tables who had opted for double bacon sandwiches. After a morning of crossing moorland in rain and howling wind, the couple were glad to warm up. This was home turf for Jasmin and she knew it didn't offer many options for refreshments; however, as her parents were meeting them later with a picnic, happily the day's cake supply was guaranteed.

After an autumn of mostly benign weather, the Pennine Way seemed intent on a proper blast of winter. Complacency in familiar terrain led to a wrong turn and a boggy climb to the summit of Black Hill. Following a family lunch, they resisted the temptation to steal Jasmin's parents' bikes and instead headed into the rain and biting wind to climb Bleaklow. After easy navigation for most of the trip, it was on the hills of Jasmin's youth that they made another error, missing Jacob's Ladder on the way to Edale Cross, resulting in a long afternoon being pelted by rain before finally arriving at the Old Nag's Head in Edale – 6 days, 8 hours and 19 minutes after leaving Kirk Yetholm.

Afterwards, they both agreed that multi-day runs give a sense of achievement you don't get from other running. 'You get such satisfaction moving from one end of the country to another without using public transport,' says Konrad, 'just getting there on your own, seeing the landscape changing as you go.'

'We love the simplicity,' says Jasmin. 'It reduces you to the essentials of what you need. All you do is run, find somewhere to sleep, eat and then run again. You can just enjoy *being* – in nature, in the surroundings and just with each other. And it's great to feel tired at the end of the day. You're hungry. Food tastes good. Bed is good. The hills are good. And you just go out and enjoy it all again the next day.

'And the wonderful thing is how many trails and routes there are out there to explore,' she adds. 'There are too many to actually do! We've got a lifetime ahead of us, lots of years. Maybe when we retire, we can do one a month!'

That evening, dripping in a corner of the pub, next to a glowing fire and having phoned the 'Dad-taxi', they had 30 minutes to wait. Plenty of time to celebrate their birthday run down the spine of England – which they did in style, with hot chocolate and, of course, slices of cake.

Further information

- Jasmin's blog: jasminfellrunner.blogspot.co.uk
- *The Pennine Way* by Paddy Dillon (Cicerone Press)

Day one, ascending Mt Whitney through the sunrise, with spectacular colours and views in every direction (Photo credit: Olly Stephenson)

SOLO IN THE SIERRAS

Fastpacking the John Muir Trail with Olly Stephenson

After another hot day, the evening air was cool and dry as Olly Stephenson hiked the Upper Basin of Kings Canyon National Park, California. He was at 3350m, 44km from the nearest trailhead, and hadn't seen another person all day. A crimson sunset streaked the horizon, daubing the surrounding peaks orange-pink. Overhead, stars began to twinkle in the inky-blue. He'd covered 50km through wonderful scenery and was ready to stop for the night.

In that moment, he felt deeply connected to the landscape and blessed to be there. The exertions of the previous day and doubt-filled night seemed a lifetime ago. Then, he had been demoralised after a demanding 65km that included climbing Mount Whitney at 4421m and Forester Pass at 4009m, carrying a full pack. If there'd been a trailhead at the first night's camp he'd have been tempted to abandon his trip, but the next morning, after a good night's sleep, he made a conscious decision to reduce his daily distances and simply enjoy the journey.

It was August 2015 and Olly was fastpacking the John Muir Trail, renowned as one of the finest long-distance hikes in the world. It typically takes backpackers three weeks to complete, with three or four resupplies along the way. It's a 355km journey, with 16,093m of ascent, through the wildest and most beautiful parts of the Sierra Nevada, between Yosemite Valley in the north and Mount Whitney in the south. The terrain is remote, with virtually no human impact, few escape routes and 10 passes over 3500m.

Olly aimed to complete the route in less than a week, to minimise time away from home, carrying all his own gear plus food for four days and planning a resupply a day or two before the end. Although a self-confessed 'ordinary bloke' and father of three, Olly is no stranger to adventure and has climbed on six continents, ridden a tandem across the USA for his honeymoon and is one of only about 50 people to have done all three classic British 24-hour fell running challenges – the Bob Graham, Charlie Ramsay and Paddy Buckley rounds.

Since he was only able to get a northbound ('NoBo') hiking permit, he had to do the highest section of the John Muir Trail first, with his pack at its heaviest, at 9kg excluding water. He was carrying an absolute minimum of kit, his reasoning being that he would always either be moving or tucked up in his sleeping bag. He'd elected to leave his stove behind to save weight and was therefore consuming cold food throughout, with his provisions in a special bear-proof Kevlar sack. His food allowance was 3750 calories per day, and after experimenting on practice trips in Scotland he was carrying four days' worth of calorie-dense food – muesli bars, peanut M&Ms,

The contents of Olly's pack laid out on his tarp at the end of his trip (Photo credit: Olly Stephenson)

Day 1, taken from near Crabtree Meadow, looking back east towards Mt Whitney (Photo credit: Olly Stephenson)

Eccles cakes, oatcakes and homemade dehydrated vegetarian meals (which were prepared using cold water and surprisingly tasty). However, despite numerous attempts to trim things down, his food had still weighed the same as the rest of his kit, each at 4.5kg.

Having little gear meant he could break camp and be away in 20 minutes; he would typically be walking by 5.30am, eating breakfast as he hiked. Mid-morning, he'd normally pass a few southbound ('SoBo') hikers labouring beneath heavy packs up one of the many mountain passes, but for the rest of the day and overnight he was usually on his own in the spectacular and enormous wilderness.

By the third morning he was fully settled into the rhythm of the trail. He packed up pre-dawn and ate his muesli from a plastic bag as he hiked. After cresting Mather Pass – the first high pass of the day – he was alone, following a thundering river and forest trails through a valley, deep in the mountains that John Muir dubbed the 'Range of Light'. His senses felt intensified as he noticed every birdsong, flower and cloud. In the heat of the day he stopped at a deep blue lake and stripped off for a dip, before stretching out on a boulder for some food and a 20-minute nap.

His plan had been to hike a few hours beyond sunset, but as he reached McClure Meadow at dusk he saw the orange glow of a campfire. Up close, he found an American hiker sat by his tent, and Olly, delighted at the prospect of a warm fire and company, decided to stay there for the night. Comparing notes, the two were both roughly at the halfway point of the 355km route, but the hiker, having taken the summer off work, was heading 'SoBo' and had taken a leisurely 40 days to get there, while Olly had taken only three – showing there are many ways to enjoy the trail.

The next night there was no warming fire. Olly wore all his running gear, including waterproofs, as he lay in his lightweight sleeping bag under his one-man tarp. He had no groundsheet, instead sleeping on a half-length mat with his shoes under his head for a pillow. After covering some extra distance, he had stopped high up on a rock slab just off the trail, rather than in a valley as on previous evenings. Here it was much colder, but as he gazed at the billions of stars pricking the sky, his only feelings were gratitude and wonder.

After four-and-a-half days he reached Reds Meadow, his planned resupply point. He hadn't eaten all his food and instead of resupplying he decided to try and eke out his remaining supplies to the end and finish in five-and-a-half days by pushing a little harder. By now his pack was much lighter and he was able to run comfortably.

That evening, Olly ate his final rehydrated dinner while hiking, before lying down to sleep by the side of the path at Thousand Lakes. At midnight, after barely two hours' sleep, he got up, determined to run through the night to the end of the trail.

In the darkness, every moth and bug illuminated by his head torch made him jump. He was aware of the risks of rattlesnakes, mountain lions and bears, and his anxieties were magnified by how small he felt in the enormous landscape. But he knew worry was pointless: even if a mountain lion were stalking him, the animal would have him in its jaws well before he'd even heard or seen it, so he may as well relax and enjoy the trail.

It was just himself, his rucksack and head torch, travelling effortlessly through the mountains beneath the starry sky. Floating down into Lyell Canyon, in the half-light

Third night, enjoying the warmth of a stranger's
compan   d campfire (Photo credit: Olly Stephenson)

of dawn, he felt pure joy. As he reached the valley floor he heard rustling behind him; he stopped and turned to see a bear standing 10 metres away, looking just as startled as he felt. They looked at each other briefly, and while Olly fumbled for his camera the animal disappeared into the trees.

Later that afternoon, for the first time on the trip, Olly ran out of water. Having dropped considerably in height, he found that some of the water sources on his map were dry due to the seven-year drought California was suffering. An American couple, out for a day-hike, had offered him some of their water, but British politeness had seen him turn it down and carry on – and then curse himself a mile further down the trail as his thirst raged. Eventually he came across a muddy pool the size of a kitchen sink, full of bugs and dirt. With 12km still to go in the heat, he knelt down with his filter, grateful to be able to fill his bottle.

He was hungry, thirsty and filthy when he arrived at the Happy Isles trailhead in the bustle of Yosemite Valley, with its campsite, shops and throngs of clean-smelling people and their myriad cars. But above all, he felt a quiet and deep satisfaction as he melted anonymously into the crowds. He had carried all his own gear and food from start to finish; all that was left over was a single packet of instant soup. He'd been totally self-sufficient, completed the route in a great time, but most importantly he'd relished his wilderness journey.

Reflecting on the trip, Olly says, 'It opened my eyes to the potential for fastpacking in the mountains and I loved it. I would encourage others to do it. It's truly one of the world's greatest long-distance hikes and it's there for everyone. You just need to do it in a way that works for you. Five-and-a-half days was perfect for me; for the next person it could be 10 or 20 days, or more.'

Olly's main advice, though, for anyone wanting to do the JMT is: 'Don't put it off. You never know what's around the corner. Don't wait until the planets are aligned to do things you've always wanted to do. Life is short and precious. It's not just about the mortgage and car and all the normal trappings of life. It's about taking time to look around you and doing things that are important to you.'

The year after his JMT, Olly fell 10 metres in a climbing accident and broke four vertebrae. Miraculously, he made a full recovery and was able to complete the 300km/25,000m La Petite Trotte à Léon race in the Alps just nine weeks later. He feels that he's been given a second chance at life. And no doubt he will use some of that precious time for new adventures, heeding the words of John Muir himself: 'Break clear away, once in a while, and climb a mountain or spend a week in the woods. Wash your spirit clean.'

Further information

- Olly Stephenson is an experienced public speaker who gives talks about his adventures. He can be contacted via Facebook or LinkedIn
- *The John Muir Trail* by Alan Castle (Cicerone Press)

A gentle warm-up outside Llanthony Priory
(Photo credit: Tori James)

FISHERMEN'S FRIENDS

Bothy-hunting in the Black Mountains with Anna McNuff

'There are people here before us,' groaned Tori.

Below them, tucked away on the riverbank, the three young women got their first glimpse of the bothy – a small red-brick building with a slate roof and green door. Wisps of smoke drifted up from the chimney and two men were moving around outside.

'What are we going to do?' asked Michelle, 'It only sleeps three!'

'Suppose we could bivvy outside,' said Anna, 'although it's freezing and it's only four o'clock. It's supposed to be minus one tonight. Maybe there's still time to get back to the car?'

It was a bright, crisp Saturday afternoon in April. Anna McNuff and her friends, Tori James and Michelle John, were on a 40km run through the Black Mountains, having planned to spend the night at Grwyne Fawr bothy halfway round. Despite being the first Welsh woman to summit Everest, Tori had never visited this bothy in her own backyard. Earlier that morning they'd collected Anna from Abergavenny where, over coffee, they'd pored over maps before choosing a route from Llanthony Priory. Anna, an adventurer, author and speaker, has run the length of New Zealand unsupported, covering 3000km in 148 days. This bothy run, however, would simply be a fun weekend away with friends.

From the priory ruins it had been a stiff climb out of the secluded Ewyas valley to pick up Offa's Dyke Path. From there, the three had been spoiled with miles of easy ridge-running along the Welsh-English border, beneath the trill of skylarks and huge skies. To the east, Herefordshire farmland glowed green and yellow with new crops, while to the west the craggy Brecon Beacons rolled into the horizon.

A qualified mountain leader, Tori had insisted they use paper maps to navigate instead of phones. In Welsh mist the plateau would have been featureless, but today they could see Hay Bluff's trig pillar in the distance as they ran and chatted – a favourite way for Anna to spend time with others.

'You get to the really good stuff when you're talking while doing things outdoors,' she says, 'like life and what you want out of it. It's a really great way to get to know people. There's something about talking and moving. You're more open and natural. You make deeper connections.'

This was not Anna's first UK running adventure; and she has also run the Jurassic Coast dressed as a dinosaur, and Hadrian's Wall as a Roman centurion. She has used these experiences in her speaking work with schoolchildren, having made video diaries about geology and Roman history along the way. Despite the chafing and the challenges of running with a heavy, mud-encrusted dinosaur tail, she says they were

Tori and Anna stop to enjoy views into the heart of Wales (Photo credit: Michelle John)

Anna and Michelle near the Twmpa with views of the Brecon Beacons (Photo credit: Tori James)

wonderful trips. And both journeys were made with friends, which is what she prefers on shorter adventures.

'It's brilliant fun to go with someone else, but I think if you want to really learn and grow or figure something out in life, then you need to go alone. On longer journeys I prefer going solo. It pushes your boundaries and you talk to more people along the way. It's a much more immersive experience. I know people who don't like being with their own thoughts, but you have to be your own best friend. You have to really like yourself, otherwise that stops so many other things in life.'

That fine spring day in the Black Mountains the three friends were far from being alone, as there were many weekend walkers out enjoying the hills. They stopped to talk to a group of teenagers on a Duke of Edinburgh expedition, labouring under heavy loads. In comparison, their own packs were compact, containing just enough gear for a night – and certainly much lighter than the 14kg Anna had carried through New Zealand, including a tent, sleeping bag and sometimes several days' food.

'New Zealand pushed me beyond anything I'd ever experienced – the isolation and discomfort.' says Anna. 'But it taught me so much. When I got to the end I was still the same person – but I now knew I could do it. Our bodies are amazing, but it's all in your head. The most important thing is self-belief. People feel they have to run fast, but I run to look at the deer and eat cake! We need to get back to the joy of running and just being outside.'

Packs were offloaded temporarily at Hay Bluff as the friends took photos and ate snacks while enjoying views of the Wye Valley and into the heart of Wales. Afterwards they dropped to Gospel Pass and then climbed the Twmpa, known locally as 'Lord Hereford's Knob'. Ahead, the escarpments rose and fell like petrified waves. Soon they turned south to follow quiet paths into the isolated valley of Grwyne Fawr, with its reservoir glinting silver in the afternoon sun. They were ready to find their home for the night.

The bothy stood next to a stream and weir. Outside, a topless man was chopping firewood, while another was in rapt concentration, adjusting a fishing rod. As the women made their way down the steep path, the pair looked up, surprised.

'Axe murderers!' whispered Michelle.

'Well, we may as well have a look round since we're here,' laughed Tori.

They chatted to the men while Anna boiled water for drinks and passed chocolate around. A patch of grey sky had appeared and begun to deliver unexpected flakes of snow. Inside, the bothy was tiny – a bare room with chairs, a stove and table, and a wooden sleeping platform above. Once a pumping house for the dam, this was the smallest of the nine MBA bothies in Wales.

Knowing about the building's previous life adds to the charm of a bothy stay for Anna. 'It was the same with Kiwi huts,' she says. 'Understanding their past teaches you about the place, its history and people. I also love that you have to think about people coming after you, as in tidying it and leaving firewood. And it's exciting that

A wood burning stove made the bothy extra cosy (Photo credit: Tori James)

you don't know who or what you'll find. It's not like you can book online or leave a TripAdvisor rating!'

The men had walked in that morning, to go fishing and take a break from their jobs as electricity linesmen. Since the pair were friendly, bothy etiquette led Tori to ask if they could also squeeze in that night.

'Sure!' they chimed. 'But it will be cosy.'

By 8pm it was dark outside. A fire spat merrily in the stove, thanks to the two men. Wrapped in hats and puffy jackets, and warmed from dinner, everyone sat around chatting. A tealight flickered in the window and wood smoke scented the air – along with something else.

'What's that smell?' said Michelle.

'My shoes!' cried Anna, diving to recover her trail shoes which had been drying by the stove.

The tongue of one of them had melted and its laces were burnt. Everyone was laughing.

'Who needs laces to run anyhow?' Anna laughed.

'This will make it better,' said Tori, pulling out a small bottle of Welsh whisky.

They all sat around the fire until midnight, sharing stories and food while listening to Mozart from one of the men's phones.

'It was as if the world didn't exist outside that bothy,' remembers Anna. 'It was actually more fun with the guys staying too. Two fishermen and three outdoors women. We would never have met otherwise!'

Eventually, four of them squeezed, top-to-toe, onto the sleeping platform, while Anna was happy to bed down on the stone floor, for extra space. She crept outside into the cold night to brush her teeth, looking at the moon and stars' reflection in the still reservoir.

The next morning the women dragged themselves from their warm sleeping bags at 8am for porridge and tea. They said goodbye to their new friends, who were already heading out to fish. From the bothy they took a different route back, over Waun Fach and through Mynydd Du Forest, running, at times in companionable silence, and not seeing another soul. Anna somehow managed in her wrecked shoes, and by lunchtime they were back at Llanthony Priory, enjoying a pub meal.

'The constantly changing scenery was amazing,' says Anna, 'but the best thing was time away with friends. And you get a taste of a big adventure in one weekend. Bothies are a great excuse for a mini-adventure. It costs nothing to stay and it's so easy. It doesn't need to be a big expedition. Just pick something you want to see and plan a route around that. Even little adventures can be life-changing.'

Anna has plenty more home-grown adventures on her bucket list. 'That's one Welsh bothy down and eight to go!' she says. 'But first, who will join me in running the West Highland Way dressed as a Highland cow?'

Further information

- Anna's website: annamcnuff.com
- Anna's epic New Zealand run is described in her book, *The Pants of Perspective* (Rocket 88 Publishing)
- Tori's website: www.torijames.com

Heading into Kintail on the Cape Wrath Ultra
(Photo credit: Louise Watson)

TO THE LIGHTHOUSE

Running the Cape Wrath Ultra, Scotland's
expedition race, with Louise Watson

Above the throb of the engine, they could hear the wail of bagpipes. Louise looked over to the shore and saw a lone piper on the jetty. Around her on deck were a hundred runners in brightly coloured gear. There was laughter and chatter, while some looked lost in their thoughts. She wondered how many would be new friends by the end of the race. Her stomach churned with a mix of excitement and nerves.

Louise Watson was on the ferry to the start of the Cape Wrath Ultra, an eight-day expedition race through northwest Scotland. Covering 400km with 11,200m of ascent, runners complete an average daily distance of 50km, with a longest day of 72km. The course largely follows the Cape Wrath Trail through tough, remote and mountainous terrain. Even for those who think they know Scotland, this is spectacular and wild country.

Even though she had completed a few ultras, this was Louise's first stage race. With a military background, she had run for over a decade, but had only grown to love it after discovering trail running with its supportive, friendly culture. Relishing a challenge, she'd entered Cape Wrath because she wasn't sure she could finish it. Also, it would take her through places she knew from childhood holidays.

'I loved the location. It was such an incredibly beautiful route,' says Louise. 'There were points where you just had to stop, that took your breath away. I felt so privileged to have the opportunity and physical ability to be there. Not everyone does. I know this from the military. I feel strongly that you have to make the most of things while you can. You just don't know what's around the corner.'

On the second afternoon of the race, she was on an undulating path next to Loch Hourn. High mountains cast shadows over the secluded valley – a scene reminiscent of Nordic fjords. Rounding a corner, she was relieved to see blue tents and marquees at the head of the loch. To applause from other runners, she crossed the line and put out her wrist and 'dibber' to a marshal. It had been a tough day, with miles of boggy track sapping her energy, but the scenery had more than compensated. Now she was ready for some chips.

After organising her gear in her allotted tent, she ate dinner and chatted with others outside. Already strong bonds were forming. 'We became a family. It was amazing to experience such stunning landscapes with such a great group of people. On day three, one of the toughest days, I dropped my sense of humour somewhere along the trail, but you can never stay miserable for long once you've reached camp.'

The event is fully supported, with a moving overnight camp, while a rolling start between 7am and 9am and a cut-off of 11pm means 16 hours for each stage, regardless of length. Participants' gear is moved for them, so they can run with just a day-pack. Despite this, many say it is harder than the Marathon des Sables, probably the world's best-known stage race, where competitors carry their own sleeping bags, water and food. At eight days, compared to five for the MdS, Cape Wrath has more long days, but its biggest challenge is the cumulative effect of over a week's running.

'The hardest thing was getting up and doing it again,' says Louise. 'On a single-stage ultra, sleep deprivation is a challenge, but you give it your best then just stop. On a stage race, there's the mental challenge of keeping going and all sorts of things suddenly become important, down to your socks and underwear! I usually run in a vest, but I got pack-rub after a day. And hydration and eating become really crucial. We were so lucky with the weather; we didn't have to manage the cumulative effect of cold and wet.'

On their fourth day, the runners dropped through Glen Torridon, bathed in sunshine – a place of childhood summers for Louise. After clambering around the lochan at the base of the Triple Buttresses, she was soon contouring the slopes, scrambling through heather, playing like a spring lamb. She dropped into a valley, which she suddenly recognised as being a place where her family used to go fishing. Alone with

Knoydart's wilderness welcoming the runners home for the night (Photo credit: Louise Watson)

the bright yellow gorse, green grass and blue sky, the intensity of the moment was almost overwhelming.

'Sometimes I feel that running is life in high definition. Everything is tuned up to the max; it's like experiencing the fullest version of life. I'm really aware of how I feel, the sensation of the weather on my skin, the noises around me. I love that feeling of heightened awareness and the simplicity of it all. It's like being tuned in and tuned out at the same time. You don't wish for anything else. You appreciate the sky, cloud and everything around you, perfect or imperfect, for what it is. And somehow that carries through to other parts of your life.'

Louise also loved the challenge of having to navigate within a 200-metre corridor of a route marked on a map: 'I'm a map and compass girl. Navigation helps me enjoy it more. It's that self-awareness, always being alert to where you are, that positive

Torridon's beauty is enhanced
in rare perfect conditions
(Photo credit: Louise Watson)

engagement with your environment, always looking and thinking. I think it helps you stay more connected with your surroundings.'

Every day required meticulous self-management and pacing to make the checkpoint cut-offs. And by day six, Louise had a new challenge – sore shins and the prospect of hours of mostly hard-packed trails. But the pain was soon forgotten as she flew down a trackless hillside into a valley. To her right, a curtain of cloud tumbled over the mountains like a waterfall. All around was empty wilderness.

'I felt my wings unfurl,' recalls Louise. 'This was what it was all about. The pain in my legs could wait. The tracks could wait. Right in that moment I felt like I was flying. I was absolutely in my element; at that moment, life was completely perfect.'

They were now in Assynt on the longest day, and with aching legs Louise was grateful for the company of fellow competitors to distract her. As they dropped into camp, they were awed by a fiery red sunset melting over the mountains and sea.

By day seven, Louise had adopted what she called the 'shin-splint shuffle' – not running, but not quite walking. Thankfully there were plentiful distractions as she ran through pure wilderness, passing seal pups and glistening lochs, accompanied by the sound of cuckoos. That evening at camp, as their first rain arrived, Louise was suddenly hit by a wave of raw emotion: 'It felt like I had crossed the finish line; I knew that if I had managed the last two days, I could make it through the final 16 miles. The highs and lows of the last seven days flooded through me. Just one more day.'

On the final morning, Louise found the soft sand a relief after miles of stony track. At 26km this was the shortest day, but with painful shins she grimaced at every step. She'd reached Sandwood Bay, a mile of golden sand with glacial-blue North Atlantic waves rolling in, guarded by a giant sea stack. Dropping to the beach, she passed three surfers who were wild camping in the grassy dunes. Beyond these lay a marshy lagoon, cradled by hills. At the end of the bay, above rocky cliffs, stretched the final section of coast to the Cape Wrath Lighthouse, the most northwesterly point in mainland Britain.

After the pristine bay came trackless terrain over peat hags and heather – which seemed an appropriate end to this wilderness journey. From the crest of the last hill, the lighthouse finally appeared. Louise quickened her pace, ignoring her battered body. She ran along a single-track road, waving to a minibus of finishers headed to the ferry. In the shadow of the lighthouse she crossed the line, to the cheers of marshals and a couple of runners. To celebrate, she opened the whisky miniature she'd carried all week. The golden liquid burned her chapped lips as the enormity of her achievement sank in.

'The sense of elation was overwhelming. I couldn't believe I'd completed such a tough event. But at same time, I didn't want it to stop. I wanted to keep going and do more.'

Of 95 runners, Louise was one of 59 finishers and fifth woman overall; but she had never been interested in times – only discovering what her limits were. 'There are so many places I want to explore through running,' she says. 'The seeds were already there, but doing the event made me see what I'm really capable of. And for me, running isn't really about running. It's about stripping life back to the bare essentials and discovering the person you really are.'

Louise's run to the tip of the country also helped cement a decision about a career change, and she has since moved to the Cairngorms to retrain as a mountain and outdoor leader. After the Cape Wrath Ultra, Louise didn't want her Scottish journey to end. It was in fact a beginning.

Further information
- Louise's blog: adventuresarecalling.me
- *The Cape Wrath Trail* by Iain Harper (Cicerone Press)
- capewrathtrailguide.org

Big grins at coming 'home' to Beinn Eighe (Photo credit: Louise Watson)

Jez running along the high trails of the Höhenweg (Photo credit: Jez Bragg)

HUT-TO-HUT ON HIGH, WILD TRAILS

Fastpacking the Tour de Monte Rosa with Jez Bragg

The valley looked a long way down. The trail was precipitous, crossing live boulder fields and scree, snaking along the mountainside at over 2000m. From afar, the route looked impassable in places – just a faint line – but in reality it wasn't so bad. There were sections of fixed rope and a narrow suspension bridge – a feat of Swiss engineering – strung across a sheer rock face. But running between red-and-white paint markers, Jez Bragg and his friend, Mike Foote, were in their element.

It was July 2014 and the two ultra-runners were on the Europaweg – a high-level, contouring trail – fastpacking the Tour de Monte Rosa in training for the UTMB, a race Jez won in 2010. A North Face sponsored athlete, Jez juggles his running with a demanding job as a construction project manager, after falling into the sport through a one-off charity marathon in 2002. Since then, Jez has won other iconic races such as the West Highland Way and Fellsman and also holds the record for running the length of New Zealand, 3054km, in just 53 days.

He had wanted to run the Tour de Monte Rosa ever since crossing it on an earlier trip, fastpacking from Zermatt to Chamonix. The route is 150km, encircling the massif on the Swiss-Italian border. With over 10,000m of ascent and passes over 2800m, it's a challenging circuit, but he and Mike planned to tackle it in three days instead of the usual 10, staying overnight in Zermatt and Alagna. His North Face teammate, Lizzy Hawker, had also spoken of the wild beauty of the area – her favourite training ground – and has since created a series of ultra-races here: the Ultra Tour Monte Rosa.

Jez uses fastpacking as training and sees it as a progression from his childhood passions, saying, 'I've been backpacking longer than running, through scouts and Duke of Edinburgh. I loved having everything on my back and being a tortoise. With a newfound love of running, I just carried on in a slightly different form – running with a lighter setup on my back, sleeping in tents and huts.'

He loves the freedom of multi-day running. 'In pure fastpacking, carrying all your stuff, it doesn't matter where you stop and sleep. If you're feeling good, you can push on into the evening and find a perfect spot on the top of a hill. There's something really special about getting out on your own two feet and seeing where and how far they will take you, and I think fastpacking takes that to another level, carrying on the next day.'

Although he enjoys self-sufficiency, his favourite trips are hut-to-hut runs. 'I got the idea for these from my first UTMB in 2005,' he says. 'It was a real eye-opener. I dragged myself around with little hill training. But I saw that there are lots of 100-mile routes in the Alps with nice trails you can run if you're lightweight. There are great huts where you can sleep and grab a meal, plus villages for resupplies. They're proper, great adventures. I've used the UTMB as an excuse to do them, splitting them into maybe two, three or four days, depending on work.'

On their second morning it was grey and damp as the pair left their hostel in Zermatt. They were concerned about the mixed forecast, since they were carrying little gear and heavy rain would mean a cold wait, sheltering in a hut. Aside from what they wore, they carried waterproofs, a spare thermal layer, capri-tights, Buffs, underwear and arm-warmers.

'We carried next to nothing. We wanted to travel as light as possible – to move as quickly as possible. It's that classic balance of fast and light, but also staying safe. The benefit of going light is you can move faster and stay warm when it's cold, without being bogged down with a heavy pack. But this is something that comes with experience and I'm lucky in that respect. You have to ask yourself – what can I get away with in terms of kit, fitness, experience, weather and remoteness of the terrain? You need to be ruthless with gear and you need experience, plus faith in your fitness, and mental strength to keep going when conditions are grim.'

As they climbed, the rain eased, the clouds parted and blue sky appeared. Jez literally jumped for joy on their first view of the Matterhorn's summit. Both felt chilly after

the wet weather, but climbing over the glaciated Theodul Pass soon warmed them up, and the novelty of running uphill on snow was a fun distraction.

From here they dropped through the Upper Cervinia ski area and past summer pastures perched high in a hanging valley, used for centuries by local farmers. At Theodul they had crossed back into Italy and Mike was excited at the prospect of Italian coffee, food and hospitality. Feeling hungry, they were soon sat outside a refuge in Resy, enjoying runner-friendly portions of polenta.

Jez prefers 'real food' when running, and instead of carrying supplies they had decided to refuel whenever the opportunity arose. With so many villages and refuges this wasn't difficult – although he got blank stares when asking about gluten-free options in a Swiss bakery!

Both loved that the route straggled two countries. 'That's part of the experience,' says Jez. 'You nip in for hot chocolate high in the mountains and chat to the locals. There's a real change in culture, people, food and language. You only have to cross the border. You always get a better coffee on the Italian side, and you'd never get pile of polenta in a Swiss refuge!'

On their last morning they left their hotel in Alagna at 6.30am. It was too early for a hotel breakfast, so it was just a banana (and unfortunately no caffeine) in anticipation of another 10-hour day. This would include just two passes, but both involved around

1600m of ascent – and to add to the challenge, Jez would have to leave Saas-Fee in his hire car at 4pm to make his flight to London.

Their first climb of the day took them on a flag-stoned path over the historic Colle del Turlo, after which they dropped to the village of Macugnaga for a late breakfast. Here, Jez attracted curious looks as he wolfed down yoghurt and a tin of peaches while sitting in the village square. Refuelled, it was up 1700m, back into Switzerland and over the final pass of Monte Moro, complete with golden Madonna. Jez loved the passes and took time to enjoy a snack and the views. That day the tops were in cloud, but they'd found the mixed weather had added to the atmosphere of being high in the mountains as they ran through dramatic cloudscapes and constantly changing skies.

They pushed on, descending to the Mattmark lake – where busloads of tourists were in contrast to the solitude and wilderness of the high trails – before the final miles to Saas-Fee.

'Tour de Monte Rosa is ideal for fastpacking and a perfect training weekend,' says Jez, 'with lovely villages to explore and get resupplies in. But it's a route that must be respected when travelling fast and light and I'd generally advise taking more time. It's advanced, but you can do it so many ways – lightweight like we did, or take a tent, carrying everything. Wild camping there would be spectacular.'

Later that evening, Jez was at Geneva airport, waiting to board his flight. Thankfully it had been delayed – otherwise he would have missed it. Even though he'd had a stressful drive there in busy traffic, he wouldn't have had it any other way.

'It's part of the adventure. I do tend to cram these trips into a weekend. Like when I was working in London and took a sleeper to Scotland, going straight from the station into the hills to fastpack the Rigby Round over two days, then home Sunday night. In the office on Mondays, when they ask what you did over the weekend, it can be impossible to explain, so I don't even go there sometimes! But it's how I've always been – drawing every last ounce out of myself.'

Fastpacking has given Jez many wonderful experiences. 'I think I've enjoyed my fastpacking adventures as training more so than the races themselves. It's the perfect excuse for a couple of weekends way – say, one in the

Playing around on the Höhenweg
(Photo credit: Jez Bragg)

Cairngorms, one in the Alps – doing long routes. And however I do them, I always have a better experience than the race itself. It's just a nicer feel to it, having more space and no time pressure. I think the appeal of racing is probably fading, and the whole solo adventure thing is becoming more and more appealing. Perhaps I'm just getting a little bit older and priorities change.'

Many of the routes he wants to explore now are closer to home – like Offa's Dyke, the Pembrokeshire Coast Path and the Southern Upland Way. And despite his love for ultra-distance, he is keen to emphasise that the activity is for everyone.

'People have this belief that it's a huge step from running round the block or 10k, to map, logistics and planning. It doesn't need to be as scary as you think. If you're creative, you can literally do something from your front door and use public transport to get back. Nothing beats a journey with a purpose. Whether it's one of those big circuits in the Alps, or a point-to-point. There's a growing thing about micro-adventures, throwing stuff in a pack and going off for a couple of days, clearing your head, camping out under the stars. It's really just getting out on your feet and exploring a bit.'

Jez is keen to share the everyday joys of running because, on his journey to becoming an elite athlete, this was always what mattered to him most. And to be alone, on foot and surrounded by beauty – this is where he feels the purest sense of freedom.

Further information
- Jez's blog: jezbragg.blogspot.co.uk
- *The Tour of Monte Rosa* by Hilary Sharp (Cicerone Press)
- Lizzy Hawker's race: www.ultratourmonterosa.com

Mike enjoying the view and a break at one of many cols on the Tour de Monte Rosa (Photo credit: Jez Bragg)

BURGH·BY·SANDS

MOORHOUSE 1½
GREAT ORTON 3½

BOWNESS 7½

KIRKANDREWS 1¾
CARLISLE 5¼

CUMBERLAND COUNTY COUNCIL

Sarah wonders which way to go
(Photo credit: Emma Timmis)

Sarah enjoying views into the heart of Northumbria (Photo credit: Emma Timmis)

ROMAN RUN

Running the Hadrian's Wall Path with Sarah Williams and Emma Timmis

'Could this be it?' said Sarah, 'After two days? Don't tell me!'

'The Wall of Hadrian!' laughed Emma, before breaking into a sprint alongside the rugged section of wall that rose like a spine from the field.

After hours in summer rain and slipping around on muddy paths, the afternoon had brightened up, and at Planetrees they had come to their first sighting of the ancient defence. Earlier that morning they had bailed out their tents after a wet night and delayed their start, hoping for better conditions. Late morning, Emma's partner, Taff, had driven them back to where they had finished the previous day and from here they ran 10km, stopping for a pub lunch before a long afternoon brought them to the remains.

It was the August Bank Holiday 2016, and Sarah Williams and her friend, the adventurer Emma Timmis, were running the Hadrian's Wall Path over five days – 136km along the World Heritage Site, across the north of England.

'I went travelling in South America after quitting my banking career in 2014,' says Sarah, 'and I kept a travel diary, with thoughts and things I wanted to do when I got home. Big and small challenges. Hadrian's Wall was on there because of that sense of history and the Romans. I'd bought the guidebook, but it had just gathered dust on my bedside table until Emma agreed to run it with me. Wine may have been involved!'

A decade earlier, Sarah's running bug had started with run-commuting: 'London was so expensive. I started running three miles to and from work. It was summer and I loved it. I saved lots of money and it's great for productivity. I love running with a purpose. From there I went on to do the London Marathon five times, then the Marathon des Sables.'

After returning from her travels she set up the 'Tough Girl Challenges' podcast, to share inspiring stories of women in adventure and sport. Her friendship with Emma, who has run across Africa twice, began after interviewing her for the show. But despite both women's running credentials, Hadrian's Wall wasn't going to be a running challenge – just time together, exploring, chatting and enjoying the countryside. In fact they had little time to train and their only preparation was looking at maps the night before starting. Taff had agreed to support them in a car so they wouldn't need to carry their camping gear, and with planning successfully avoided, they were off.

By 9am on their third morning they were wandering around the ruined Temple of Mithras, the Sun God, at Carrawburgh Fort. It was a bright, cool day and the terrain was much hillier here. They'd reached Northumberland National Park, where the wall's remains are best preserved. At the end of an aisle they peered into two altars which visitors had filled with flowers and coins. They were 5km into what would be their longest day, at 34km, and their shoes, which had dried overnight, were already soaked from wet grass.

'The area was much more beautiful than I ever expected,' says Emma. 'It was like a classic painting of the English countryside – rolling hills, sheep, farmhouses and drystone walls. It was stunning. Without Sarah suggesting it, I would probably never have explored this part of the country.'

From the fort, the two were soon running and walking the rollercoaster path that clings to the edge of the Whin Sill escarpment on basalt cliffs,

At last! Emma arriving at the ancient wall
(Photo credit: Sarah Williams)

enjoying spectacular views into the empty, wild heart of Northumbria. They passed the remains of more forts and some lookouts, then dropped steeply to Sycamore Gap, where a handsome, lone tree stands in a gulley, close to the roman milecastle known as Castle Nick, looking like a rounded sheepfold. This is one of the most photographed points on the path, made famous in the film *Robin Hood, Prince of Thieves*.

Seeing the landscape change is one of the things Sarah enjoys most about multi-day running. 'I prefer point-to-point runs to doing a loop. You experience such varied scenery. And you just get into this flow. You get to a point where you don't need to think anymore. Life becomes very simple. Especially on the MDS – you wake up, dress, run, drink water, take your salt tablets, get to the next checkpoint. All your decisions are made.'

And for Sarah, running is nourishment for the spirit. 'I love getting outside, seeing sky, greenery, hearing the birds. It resets you. Just switching off. Decompressing in nature. It's so good for the soul, for your physical and mental wellbeing.'

A little later they met Taff at a car park. They dried their shoes in the sun and enjoyed a picnic to the sound of his guitar playing – he was enjoying plenty of practice while he acted as support crew. With only a rough plan of how far they wanted to run each day, Taff was driving ahead to find a campsite and set up tents.

'It was really nice to have a support team,' says Sarah, 'especially as I've done so many things when it's just been me, by myself. And it was good to do a trip without as much planning as I'd normally do – to just go with the flow, see how we felt and see what would happen. It was great to play it by ear for a change.'

That evening, their relaxed approach allowed Taff to surprise them. Instead of a campsite, he'd found a bunkhouse for the night – a cosy, converted barn on a farm in Gilsland. With hot showers, comfy beds and home-baked treats, it felt like a luxury break in a spa.

The next afternoon they stumbled across more treats as they encountered, pathside, the 'Stall on the Wall' – a crate full of biscuits, chocolate, crisps and drinks, with a price list and honesty box. Already buzzing with sugar due to the large slices of cake they'd had at lunchtime, they walked away from the hoard empty-handed. Unfortunately they were now walking more than running due to Sarah having a sore foot, but this was not about to spoil their trip.

'The thing I love about an adventure is that even if you don't complete it the way you planned, it's still an adventure!' says Emma. 'Walking meant we were able to talk more as we weren't pushing our bodies so hard. We had some great brainstorming sessions, got to know each other better and develop our friendship. It turned out to be really therapeutic. Fresh air and exercise inspires creative thinking. Going at a slower pace, we were also able to take in more of our surroundings, see the amazing views and chat to people we met.'

On the afternoon of their final day, the views softened to an expanse of green salt marsh as they walked the final miles along the Solway Firth. Across the water they could see, only three miles away, houses in Scotland. Birds waded among the reeds and big clouds scuttled overhead. A wooden shelter marked the end of the path, where they found the box and last ink stamp to mark the souvenir passports they were carrying, to record their journey across the top of the Roman Empire.

'Just do it!' says Sarah. 'Just get the guidebook or the map. Navigation is super-easy. Just pick a date and go. The back of that *Hadrian's Wall Path* book has all the other national trails listed. We're so lucky. It's planted a seed. Wouldn't it be amazing to do all of them – especially if you took 10 years, doing one trail each summer? It would be a great way to explore the UK and see more of our amazing countryside!'

'It was an awesome trip,' agrees Emma. 'Short and pretty manageable for most people, even with varying fitness levels.'

She smiles before adding, 'But as with all the adventures I've ever had, my favourite thing was just having a laugh with a great friend.'

Further information
- Sarah's website: www.toughgirlchallenges.com
- Emma's website: www.emmatimmis.com
- *Hadrian's Wall Path* by Mark Richards (Cicerone Press)

Finished! At the end of the Hadrian's Wall Path at Bowness-on-Solway (Photo credit: Sarah Williams)

Fleeing the Tour du Mont Blanc crowds on Crête des Gittes in the Beaufortain, Savoie (France) (Photo credit: Rosie Sargisson)

THE FASTPACK JOURNALS

Exploring the world through multi-day running with Rosie Sargisson and Jeff Fong

'I love the meditative quality of trail running. You just run and stop thinking about anything else,' says Rosie Sargisson. 'You work really hard to get to a summit, and I'm not religious, but you get this spiritual feeling. The Earth is just incredibly beautiful. I never get that feeling in the city. Even skiing on a mountain, there are people all around and you're using chairlifts, so it doesn't do the same for me. But when you do it yourself and you're the only engine to get to some of these places, suddenly they become so much more beautiful.'

It was their love of running that inspired the decision by Rosie and her partner, Jeff Fong, to take a career break and fastpack some of the world's best long-distance trails. The pair originate from New Zealand, and jaded by three years of corporate life in Singapore, they left their jobs to see the world and assess their futures. They'd previously escaped the city to compete in day-long races in Malaysia, Mongolia, Vietnam and China and this led to the idea of combining travel and running.

They chose Europe for their time away because of its variety, quality of trails and plentiful accommodation that would make it easier to travel 'fast and light'.

Testing times in the Kamnik–Savinja Alps, Slovenia (Photo credit: Jeff Fong)

Fastpacking in New Zealand or the USA, you might have to carry several days' provisions, camping gear and maybe even plan for bears! After many hours of internet research by Jeff, their final itinerary comprised a month in each of five different countries – Scotland, France, Norway, Slovenia and Turkey – after a first month at home in New Zealand, rediscovering local routes by fastpacking them.

'Keep your pack as light as possible,' is Rosie's advice for anyone trying fastpacking for the first time. 'A heavy pack can really ruin your day.'

They carried minimal gear, chosen either because it was super-lightweight or wouldn't smell after several days' wear, and they ate cold food when camping. Their nutritional strategy was to carry fat- and protein-dense food for the highest calorie-to-weight ratio.

In Scotland, from where Rosie's family had emigrated generations earlier, they developed a love affair with the humble oatcake while running the West Highland Way and the Skye Trail. They ate hundreds, slathered in peanut butter – getting through eight jars in one month! But it wasn't always sparse dining. Immersing themselves in the local cultures, they enjoyed eating in Alpine mountain huts; and in Slovenia their trail running journey morphed into 'The Food and Wine Tour of Southeastern Slovenia' as they sampled local fare while running through the country's fruit bowl.

Here, they were running the Slovenska Planinska Pot trail, which traverses the width of the country widely known as 'Europe-in-miniature'. Despite a terrifying incident with loose rock on a chain-and-cable aided section, Rosie's confidence in tackling technical terrain grew massively during the trip. Jeff thinks it has taught them much about their capabilities and he loved exploring through running. 'The best thing was we did it all ourselves. We organised it and ran it ourselves. We propelled ourselves across Slovenia. We propelled ourselves halfway down the French Alps. It was a huge adventure!'

Jeff's tip for new fastpackers is to be patient and understand that you won't always be able to run. 'Don't beat yourself up if you're not running. You're carrying this heavy bag and you're going a long way. There will be times when you walk and that's OK!'

In France, on the GR5, there was certainly a lot of walking as they took on huge Alpine passes, sometimes covered in snow, even in summer. But the reward for their efforts was that they often enjoyed total solitude – a welcome contrast to busy Singapore, with its long work hours and consumerist culture. For Jeff, this unique way of experiencing the natural world is what makes fastpacking special. 'You usually get to have the whole mountain to yourself. You get a great feeling and connection with the outdoors – especially because you're doing it for such a long period of time – which you don't really get if you run for a day, or if you're just entering a race.'

The French Alps were spectacular and marred only by serious snoring in one of the mountain refuges, but the pair both loved hut-to-hut running and the simplicity of life on a multi-day journey. 'It's how I imagine living life back in time,' Rosie says. 'It feels more like you're experiencing what it's like to be human, rather than the human construct of society. So instead of working in a job, to meet targets and make money, you may not be hunting animals but you use your body and see what your body can really do. And because you're staying in huts, you have this social, tribal environment where everyone is doing the same thing. It's a kind of pure life. I really like it.'

They also feel strongly that with the pressure to share every athletic endeavour on Strava and the like, running the routes just for fun and exploration allowed them to discover the joy of running for its own sake – not for competition, times or staying in shape. Jeff says, 'While we did update our blog and Instagram, we also made a concerted effort to be disconnected. In an age when everyone posts everything online, there's always a bit of a battle, because you want to share things that are cool. But it became important for us to do something just for ourselves.'

While he finds it impossible to choose a favourite country, a highlight for Jeff was Norway's Ryfylkestien trail, where they enjoyed remote, pristine wilderness, rarely encountering people or road in two weeks. Here, they wild camped and to stay light they ate tinned mackerel and butter crackers. Although it was August, there was still snow around, and their nights were bitterly cold, even sleeping fully dressed. Towards the end of their trip, they finally decided to try some of the renowned Nordic huts.

Full of smiles on the Ryfylkestien, Norway (Photo credit: Jeff Fong)

With people walking away from the Skapet cabin, it didn't look likely that there would be space to stay, but it transpired that the hut had been opened that very afternoon by Norway's health minister, with a party, 500 guests and live band – all of whom had left afterwards. The place was deserted apart from six staff, and Rosie and Jeff were led to their own private cabin, straight out of the pages of a Nordic design magazine, with freshly made beds and floor-to-ceiling views of the fjords and mountains. They couldn't believe their luck.

Later one of the hut staff knocked on the door. 'We've got too much food, would you like dinner?' The two didn't need to think before answering. In a cosy dining room, by a wood fire, they were fed a three-course meal and poured red wine. 'The full bottles would be extra weight for the helicopter to take out!' The next morning they were given breakfast – the homemade bread was destined for the bin otherwise.

Local bread and baking became a new passion inspired by all the countries they visited. The political situation in Turkey resulted in plans to run the Lycian Way being replaced by a month in Crete, which gave them a chance to live in a small, rural community, run the local trails unencumbered by a pack, and learn to bake new loaves every day.

Their time away has allowed the couple to reassess their priorities. 'We'd already started buying less and not wanting so much stuff,' says Rosie. 'When you have a small pack, you can't add to it, so you don't buy touristy knick-knacks and you only take away memories or photos. My desire to consume has definitely decreased, and my awe of the environment and its importance has grown massively. Now I'd rather use money and time for experiences. It's made me really value people and experiences and a sense of community and a sense of belonging.'

Jeff adds, 'I think it's helped us to assess what's really important – especially having had all these amazing experiences. We really want to fit those into our lives somehow. We've decided for now, at this stage of our lives, that a corporate trajectory isn't for us, so it's looking like we'll go home and try to open a bakery.'

Fastpacking has given the couple adventures on some of the world's best long-distance paths. Perhaps it has also set them on a new path in life.

Further information
- Jeff & Rosie's blog: www.fastpackjournal.com
- *The GR5 Trail* by Paddy Dillon (Cicerone Press)
- *The West Highland Way* by Terry Marsh (Cicerone Press)
- *Trekking in Slovenia* by Justi Carey, Roy Clark (Cicerone Press)
- *Walking in Norway* by Constance Roos (Cicerone Press)
- *The Skye Trail* by Helen & Paul Webster (Cicerone Press)

Whiteout conditions justified the inclusion of goggles and crampons on the kit list (Photo credit: © 2017 Spine® Race & Spine® Challenger. Photographer Yann Besrest Butler)

A GREAT BRITISH ADVENTURE

Running 'The Spine', Britain's most brutal race, with Iain Harper

In pitch-black woods, flashes of torchlight illuminated bare trees and drizzle. Descending the steep, muddy gully, it was impossible to stay upright. Curses rang through the darkness whenever one of them fell. This was an unforgiving end to a tough first day. Iain Harper and his race partner, Steve Jefferson, eventually came out at Hebden Hey Scout Centre. It was 3.30am on a Sunday and they'd covered over 40 miles in 16 hours.

Brutal January weather had delayed the start; people were being blown over. At Kinder Downfall the wind was blowing the waterfall back uphill, soaking runners as they passed. They ran through sleet, blizzards, 80mph winds, and hail that had caused eye injuries for some. Just before the M62 motorway bridge they were handed hot drinks by some marshals.

'It was then I started to appreciate just how much we take for granted,' recalls Iain. 'That solitary cup of tea meant everything at that moment. We grabbed some food and crossed the motorway. I remember looking down at the cars whipping by below, wondering where their drivers were going. I thought of the warm beds they'd be sleeping in and the families they'd be returning to. In 25 years of winter mountain experience, those were the worst conditions I've ever experienced.'

*Icy descents pile on the pain
(Photo credit: © 2017 Spine®
Race & Spine® Challenger.
Photographer Yann Besrest Butler)*

It was January 2015 and Iain was among 240 people running the Spine Race, a 268-mile single-stage winter ultra-marathon along the length of the Pennine Way. He is CEO of a start-up, author of Cicerone's guide to the *Cape Wrath Trail* and an ultra-runner – an evolution of his extreme backpacking, such as on midwinter expeditions to the Northwest Highlands while researching his book.

Looking for a new challenge after completing the Lakeland100 with Steve, they chose the Spine. The seed had perhaps been planted years earlier, while backpacking in the Peak District, when Iain had chatted to an elderly park volunteer. 'He told me that as a boy he'd taken part in the 1932 Kinder Trespass with his father,' says Iain. 'As we headed to our wild camp in the afternoon sun, I reflected on how much we take for granted. Just a generation-and-a-half ago our rights and freedom to roam were far from secure.'

The Pennine Way was the UK's first designated national trail and 2015 was its 50th anniversary. The Spine bills itself as 'Britain's most brutal race', with hypothermia and frostbite being very real dangers. Usually only a third of entrants finish the event. Although the race is run continuously, there are five checkpoints where runners can get a hot meal and sleep – but, with the clock ticking, the temptation to push on is strong. With a young son, busy job and post-graduate studies, training had been difficult and Iain had felt daunted and woefully unprepared at the start.

The scout hut was an explosion of people, wet clothing and muddy footwear. Movement inside was chaotic. Every space was crammed with kit or runners. Iain recovered his makeshift drop-bag – his wife's flowery suitcase, which had caused much hilarity, but was at least easy to find. While runners also had the option of bivvying or camping en route, Iain and Steve had decided to use the checkpoints as places to sleep and sort gear for the next stage. After a shower and food, Iain found an empty bunk, but sleeping was difficult – even with an eye mask and earplugs. A little later, after devouring two breakfasts and coffee, they continued into a cold, rainy dawn.

The second stage to Hawes, Checkpoint 2, was the longest at 60 miles, but they decided to stop and bivvy around Checkpoint 1.5 at Malham Tarn. En route, it was a welcome relief to reach the pub at Lothersdale.

'There was a roaring fire and the landlord had turned the pool room into a makeshift checkpoint,' recalls Iain. 'We had tea and hot food as our kit steamed on the radiators. Leaving there was hard. So much so that we stopped at the next pub in East Marton too! The Sunday evening crowd looked bemused as we shed our kit. When we told them what we were doing, the landlady made a donation to Steve's JustGiving page and they sent us on our way with warm wishes, encouragement and crisps!'

They decided that to also stop at the pub in Gargrave would constitute a pub-crawl, so they pushed on until 2am when they searched for a bivvy spot in Malham, finding only the public toilets open. 'There were German competitors in the ladies, so Steve and I bagged the gents. I drew the short straw and got the urinal end. I crawled

Spectacular sunset on the Spine following a bleak day (Photo credit: Iain Harper)

into my bivvy bag and pretty much passed out. We'd agreed two hours' sleep, but it felt like just 10 minutes later when we had to leave.'

Pulling on wet gear and leaving in darkness and rain was a real low point for the pair. Boggy fields and slippery limestone took them to Malham Tarn Field Centre, where runners were asleep, heads on tables. They were held there for an hour due to atrocious weather before being released into screaming wind, so strong it supported their entire body weight. Encased in Gore-Tex, Iain's reality became a tiny cleft of vision between the top of his balaclava and his hood. With 100mph winds forecast, they were diverted from Pen-y-Ghent onto a low-level route to Horton-in-Ribblesdale, where the café was doing a roaring trade in bacon sandwiches.

Following a magenta sunset, they arrived on Monday night in Hawes, where, stunned and exhausted, they were looked after by volunteers who brought them their drop-bags, food and tea. 'One of Steve's friends brought fish and chips,' says Iain. 'The hardship seems to enhance your enjoyment of everyday pleasures. I don't think I've ever enjoyed a chip quite as much. After eating, I decided to sleep before kit faffing; I found a cupboard off the main room and laid out my Therm-a-Rest!'

From Hawes, concerned about cut-offs, they set off at a brisk pace. At this point they needed micro-spikes on the treacherous, icy ground. They were aiming for the Tan Hill Inn, the highest pub in England, where coincidentally Steve got married.

'Competitors spoke of Tan Hill as a warm oasis open all hours,' says Iain. 'My mind conjured images of a roaring fire and hot food. When we arrived at 5am the reality was very different: the pub was shut tight and we crowded into a cramped porch to get out of the snow. I tried to eat a bit but started to get cold, so we set off at a real lick. OS maps describe an area near there as simply 'The Bog' – and they're not wrong!'

Early on Tuesday afternoon they reached Middleton-in-Teasdale, Checkpoint 3, where they stopped for seven hours of much-needed rest. After that, despite leaving in the early hours in ankle-deep snow, they missed the cut-off for the high route over High Cup Nick and Cross Fell. Now, thinking the low route would be easy, Iain let down his guard. He stopped eating and even fell asleep briefly while walking. 'Passing through Garrigill there were lots of rabbits hopping about on the village green,' laughs Iain. 'Neither of us mentioned them at the time for fear that we were hallucinating. It was only much later we admitted we'd both seen them.'

A blur of cold, hunger and exhaustion led them to Alston, arriving at 4am. Here, the race was paused for 24 hours due to the 100mph winds. They were glad to rest but soon felt claustrophobic as cabin fever set in after days of solitude. The centre was packed with marshals and competitors. Runners prowled around like hungry jackals and everyone was relieved to set off again at 6am on the Thursday morning.

Day merged into night into day. The only constants were moving forward plus surviving the weather and landscape. However, another dimension was added as they approached Hadrian's Wall.

'I'd been particularly looking forward to that section,' says Iain. 'The ancient green sward of turf stretching out in front of us belied the history of the place. There was a special feeling looking down over jutting stone abutments, sharing the same view as those here thousands of years before. The Spine Race induces its own sense of timelessness. Here, the huge span of history made the experience even more otherworldly.'

From the Wall, Iain's friend, Simon, would be supporting them. As driving rain and wind pursued them, they made the mistake of not eating. On reaching Simon's car, Iain was borderline hypothermic and he had to recover inside, with heaters on full-blast, before continuing through soul-destroying bog to Bellingham. This was the last checkpoint and their spirits were low. As Iain lay down under a table to sleep, finishing seemed impossible.

On waking he still felt rubbish, but it was a beautiful, crisp day. Flagstones made route-finding easier but these were covered in ice. Steve had mislaid his micro-spikes and in this final leg, for the first time, lost his sense of humour as they tackled treacherous, icy descents. By nightfall they were on the last 27-mile stretch along a ridge. Cold and tired, Iain ran out of water and stopped at unfrozen rivulets to glug water like a desert wanderer.

Sleep deprivation was playing with his mind: 'In a semi-delirious state I thought I was having a heart attack on the final climb into Kirk Yetholm. I remember trying to calculate whether an aneurysm would prevent me from crawling the last mile to the Border inn. That's what this race does to you!'

Arriving late Thursday night in the town, the pair eventually saw a small group of headlights and people beckoning them. They made a painful lope along the road until they touched the wall at the Border pub, 268 miles, 133 hours and 18 minutes after starting.

'The scale of the race makes it hard to process mentally,' reflects Iain, 'but little by little I started to piece the race back together. Hour by hour, step by step it became a coherent whole – a body of memory that will abide with me for the rest of my life. An experience so much more precious than any material possession. We were there that wild week in January when the Pennine Way turned 50. And we did something that only a few others will ever do and that only we will ever fully understand.'

*The coveted finishers' patch and medal
(Photo credit: Iain Harper)*

Further information
- thespinerace.com
- *The Pennine Way* by Paddy Dillon (Cicerone Press)

From a camp in Bhutan, looking through a pass towards Tibet (Photo credit: Chris Ord)

IN THE LAND OF THE THUNDER DRAGON

Trail running in the Kingdom of Bhutan with Anna Frost

Tourists labouring up the zig-zag path were bemused as the runners passed them, all dressed in bright colours and powering up the steepest sections with hands on knees. At 900m above the Paro Valley floor their destination, the Tiger's Nest Monastery, clung to the side of a cliff jutting from the forested mountainside. This has been a site of meditation since the eighth century, and that day's route was the perfect pre-lunch acclimatisation run for a group that included Anna Frost, the New Zealand-born international mountain- and ultra-runner.

It was October 2015 and Anna was co-leading a trail-running trip in Bhutan with her Australian friend, Chris Ord, a consultant in adventure tourism and founder and editor of *Trail Run Mag*. Anna is an ambassador for SisuGirls, an empowerment project whose aim is to get girls outside and help them reach their potential. As well as iconic ultras like Hardrock 100 and Transvulcania, Anna has won multi-stage races such as the five-day Costa Rica Coastal Run and the seven-stage Manaslu Mountain Trail in Nepal. She also holds the women's record for the Everest Marathon, which she won in 2009 despite being chased and knocked down by a yak 2km before the end.

Known as 'the last Shangri-La', the tiny Buddhist kingdom of Bhutan has been shrouded in mystery for centuries, and for nine runners this would be the trip of a lifetime. Their eight-day expedition run would follow the first half of the Snowman Trek, reputed to be the world's toughest hike. This was the first time such a run had been attempted and much of their 170km journey would be over 4000m, reaching a high point of 5005m, in remote, raw wilderness.

The pristine landscapes of Bhutan are comparatively untouched due to the country's tourism policies. For visitors, open travel across the country is forbidden; their numbers are capped and each must pay a fixed daily charge of $250, which covers a guide, food and accommodation. These factors eliminate the usual backpacker crowd and with most people coming to trek, trail running is uncommon in the country. Moving a group of runners along a remote, high-altitude route, at double the pace of hikers would be a new challenge for the local support crew. 'They are beginning to understand running more,' says Anna, 'although until Chris and I came with a group no one had really experienced it before. But many of our crew were really liberated by the trip and there is much more running in the country now.'

The Himalaya region holds a special place in Anna's heart. 'Running in Bhutan is tough, technical, muddy, extremely high altitude and cold. But it's incredibly stunning which makes it all worth the hard yards,' she says. 'And being in Bhutan and Nepal always reminds me of things to be grateful for. The simple things in life that really matter. The size of us humans compared to beautiful, powerful Mother Nature. It is always good to be brought back to basics.'

After three days of acclimatisation, the group made the four-hour jeep journey up Paro Valley to the trailhead. Joining them there were their mules and crew – a guide, mule handlers, cooks, camp managers and porters. Their first day took them next to the raging Paro River, over rickety bridges and through dense, ancient forest to reach their overnight camp. Bhutan has strong environmental laws which require 60% of its natural landscapes to be forested. Impressively, 72% remains untouched and the country is carbon negative. This results from its policy of 'Gross National Happiness' which seeks to increase its citizens' wellbeing and ensure that development does not come at the cost of the environment, culture or society.

While some Bhutanese no doubt struggle to balance a Buddhist approach with the material temptations of the West, the nation as a whole appears to have found a middle way. 'The effect of Gross National Happiness there is undeniable,' says Anna. 'It's extremely strong. You see a spiritual and enlightened way of life everywhere you walk. It's really special and wonderful to be around. And running in Bhutan is as impressive and even more untouched than a lot of the trails in Nepal. The people are always ready to help, with a huge smile on their face.'

For days the group ran through vast, wild mountain landscapes, occasionally passing isolated villages with terraced fields and the glint of a white chorten (Buddhist shrine). Sometimes they encountered nomadic yak herders who tried to sell them

Anna springing up towards a pass at 4870m (Photo credit: Chris Ord)

Running the highest pass at 5000 metres with Jomolhari in the background (Photo credit: Chris Ord)

A perched village on the Snowman Trek (Photo credit: Chris Ord)

yak's cheese or jars of dried caterpillars with mushroom heads – a local delicacy resulting from a fungus infecting the larvae. Considered an aphrodisiac, these have a huge market in China, and have made the locals wealthy in relative terms.

Often the group power-walked the steep, rocky paths. Their pace meant plenty of time for photos and their effort was rewarded with views of 7326m Jomolhari, among other summits. 'Every day we had breathtaking views,' says Anna. 'It was just magical running around a corner and facing another 7000m mountain range. To feel so small, to see such huge virgin mountains, reminded us how precious our world is.'

Although they were only covering a modest 20–30km a day, it was slow going, but they were happy to pick their way carefully along the trails. The extreme remoteness of the route meant that injury or illness would result in serious problems, with no quick or easy way out – despite having a spare mule for emergencies. As it was, the thin air made running difficult even when they did find level, contouring trails.

'Altitude was the main issue that everyone had to deal with,' says Anna. 'Acclimatisation is essential and you need to listen to your body for any warning signs of altitude sickness. The biggest challenge of leading a group there is making sure that everyone is feeling OK and keeping on top of that.'

Ironically, it was group leader, Chris, and another Australian runner, who suffered the most altitude symptoms – even though they'd prepared with training sessions in a special chamber that simulated the reduced oxygen conditions. It's not high mileage that's needed to prepare for this kind of trip, but leg strength for the climbing and the ability to recover quickly, to continue the next day. Thankfully there were no serious issues, but the altitude, technical trails and lack of facilities made this a challenging undertaking, even fully supported.

On their fifth evening they were in a high, wild, rocky meadow at Robluthang, surrounded by pristine peaks, and a cluster of brightly coloured tents formed the night's camp – tents for sleeping, dining, cooking and one for the toilet. The mules grazed nearby while the runners, cocooned in puffy jackets, waited for dinner below the setting sun, clutching mugs of tea and sharing stories. Lunch had been hours earlier, when they'd caught up with the porters on the trail who were carrying curries kept warm in insulated containers.

Anna enjoys the camp life experienced on stage races and in expedition running. 'I love the social aspect of multi-day races,' she says. 'Camping and eating all together, sleeping under the same stars and waking the next day to push again on the same trails.'

That night's valley was a mass summer migration point for takin, Bhutan's national animal – a goat-antelope, sometimes known as a gnu goat – but it was too late in the season to see them. There is, however, plentiful wildlife in Bhutan, including tigers, snow leopards and black-necked cranes, due to huge efforts in conservation. 'The mountains are the main attraction there,' says Anna. 'They are enormous and stunning and untouched. Wildlife is a little more sacred; you have to go to specific jungles to see the panda and bears, but we saw lots of yaks and blue sheep, plus evidence of mountain lions with fresh kill – although we didn't have any sightings.'

After eight days of sky-high running, the party finally dropped to the village of Gasa, the end of their journey, where they could sample hot springs and enjoy showers and a proper bed. It was also a chance to celebrate a tough and unforgettable journey that few people are lucky enough to make. Despite its fierce reputation, everyone successfully managed the route. Anna reflects, 'There was so much joy afterwards in seeing the look of achievement on people's faces.'

Anna's athletic career has led her onto podiums around the world, but at heart it's not the winning that matters to her. 'Through running,' she says, 'I simply love to explore what's around the next corner, over the next hill; to be free in nature and to push my own physical limits.'

Further information
- Anna's blog: frostysfootsteps.wordpress.com
- Running tours with Anna: www.trailrunadventures.com
- Bhutan and other trail running tours: www.tourdetrails.com
- *Trekking in Bhutan* by Bart Jordans (Cicerone Press)

Full of smiles on the Pennine Way
(Photo credit: Chris Wren)

FOLLOWING IN THE FOOTSTEPS OF SPRING

A journey from Land's End to John O'Groats with Aly Wren

Aly Wren and Malcolm Bassett crouched in a corner of the cross-shaped wall, shel-tering from winds that had battered them since leaving Dufton. It had been a tough climb to the top of Cross Fell, England's highest point outside Cumbria. In the pub the previous evening they had both been unusually quiet, despite a glorious day that had taken them past High Force, finishing with the spectacular rift of High Cup Nick lit by shafts of sunlight. Both had been apprehensive about the next day's route – relatively short at 32km, but with a poor weather forecast.

From their packs they pulled out squashed croissants – a surprise from the hostel warden – and their one regular luxury: a small flask of tea, usually shared after the first 10 miles. Refreshed, they surfaced from the lee of the wall and took in a final view of the Eden Valley and distant English Lakes. 'Let's get out of here!' shouted Aly, and they flew down the rough track known locally as the Corpse Road, heading for Alston below.

It was May 2009 and Aly and Malcolm were on the Pennine Way section of their charity Land's End to John O'Groats run. For Aly, running has been a way of life since being treated for thyroid cancer 30 years ago. Following surgery, she trained in the hope that building her physical strength would aid recovery. In the process, she astonished her consultants by placing third in the Yorkshireman Off-Road Marathon during her chemotherapy, in spite of low blood counts. They quickly became some of her biggest supporters.

It was through running she met Malcolm and they soon became the best of friends and trail companions. Over the past decade the pair, along with others from Hinckley Running Club, have run many of the UK's long-distance trails, with minibus support, over an annual weekend away. Inspired by an article about the iconic LEJOG route, they were hooked by the idea of making the journey themselves, but staying off-road and taking in places they wanted to see.

'It's perfectly feasible to design your own route, so long as you're sensible about distances,' says Aly. 'Most importantly, allow yourself plenty of time to enjoy it – to look around and take everything in. Those memories last a lifetime. And enjoy the planning. When you come to run it, it's like the story starts to unfold right before your eyes!'

Poring over OS maps every Monday evening for 10 months, they devised a route that would see them on the South West Coast Path; crossing Dartmoor in a day; picking up the Macmillan Way to the Cotswolds; running through Derbyshire; joining the Pennine Way to the Borders; crossing central Scotland to the West Highland Way; then running through the Great Glen before turning north to John O'Groats. They planned seven weeks for the journey, booking accommodation for every night of the trip – 18 youth hostels and 30 B&Bs. Both had taken a sabbatical from their jobs and there was no contingency in their schedule. 'We had to go out believing we could do it,' says Aly. 'If anything had gone wrong we'd basically have had to abort the trip.'

As it turned out, they had surprisingly few issues – just odd niggles, sunburnt ears, and bizarrely, Aly caught her hand on some giant hogweed, unaware that its sap reacts with sunshine, resulting in ulcerated skin. 'People were fascinated with my blackening finger. But thankfully it wasn't serious!'

They had prepared with back-to-back training weekends, often running 30 miles to Hathersage Youth Hostel and back the next day. But mostly they were relying on their bodies getting stronger as they progressed. For the first two weeks, twitchy legs disturbed their sleep, but this soon stopped and a daily marathon became normal to them.

'Bodies are amazing in what they can do,' says Aly. 'I really wish, especially for young women today, that we'd celebrate good, strong bodies instead of what we see in magazines; that we'd value fitness and strength and how our bodies can carry us to the tops of hills and mountains and to all these wonderful places!'

By day 31 they had reached Northumbria and it was a cool, spring morning as they climbed out of Byrness, passing wild goats that were grazing the hillsides.

Enjoying some flowing single-track in Linlithgow (Photo credit: Chris Wren)

Soon they were running over a lovely, rolling expanse of soft green, with Malcolm bounding ahead of Aly, when, with a yelp, he suddenly disappeared waist-deep into the ground. Unbeknown to either of them, they had entered an area of sphagnum moss, carpeting a peat bog. When she'd stopped laughing, Aly lay on a patch of solid ground and pulled him out, with a champagne cork pop as his legs reappeared. Finding the main path, they continued, but an hour later, peering over a fence at some spotted toadstools, Malcolm suffered an electric shock – to more laughter and little sympathy. But despite Malcolm's mishaps, the Cheviots was one of their favourite places on the whole journey.

'It was an area I'd never really explored, that edge of Northumberland into Scotland, and it was stunning and unspoilt – like some of the wilderness you go further north for. There was a lot of climbing but you were often surrounded by a panorama of wild, green hills. It was like finding a jewel you weren't expecting.'

On the shores of Loch Ness, on day 42 of their journey, they pushed open the door of the youth hostel. Strung to their bulging rucksacks were bags containing dinner ingredients – pasta, sauce, cheese, bread and chocolate – which they'd bought in the village store in Invermoriston. Throughout much of their trip, friends and family had provided support and some had even run stages with them, but for four days, as they followed the Great Glen before heading north to the coast at Dornoch, they were alone. The pair were carrying all their own gear, waterproofs, spare lightweight shoes, and a second set of running kit they'd wear that evening after handwashing that day's clothes. Starting each day by 8.30am and finishing in the early afternoon would allow plenty of time for recovery and to review the next day's maps.

As they cooked dinner, they were surprised when the warden said there was a phone call for them. It was Carolyn, a woman they'd met weeks earlier at the foot of Pen-y-Ghent, who coincidentally lived in nearby Drumnadrochit and had been following their progress on the website that Aly's son was updating daily. She insisted on delivering their gear the next day to their guesthouse in Beauly, allowing them to travel light. Alongside this, she also left a bag of chocolate and treats. 'She was one of our many guardian angels,' says Aly. 'We were overwhelmed by the support we had along the way.'

A further joy was their extended springtime, following it north through the country. When they'd left Cornwall its woods had been flooded with bluebells; they had continued to enjoy these through Yorkshire, then on the shores of Loch Lomond, and nearly seven weeks later in a perfect purple meadow at Dunrobin Castle. From here, they ran past seal pups basking on empty beaches by the North Sea and waded across an estuary at Sinclair's Bay, before finally reaching John O'Groats 49 days and 1208 miles after they started.

Freshening up tired legs in Lower Slaughter, the Cotswolds (Photo credit: Chris Wren)

'It was the journey of a lifetime,' says Aly. 'There's so much to explore in the UK. People don't realise how beautiful our country is. I just love the adventure of getting from A to B on my own two feet. It's amazing that you might start the day, say, in a forest and later you're looking down onto a glorious valley and all that climbing was down to you. Sometimes I'd stop, turn around and look at where I'd come from and go, "Wow – how can I have covered all of that?"'

'And I loved the wildlife,' she adds. 'Seeing mountain hares, beautiful birds of prey and the flowers. It's like we were part of the landscape. Everything else just ceased to exist; you're completely at home, running through it, just enjoying it and taking it all in.'

Through their epic run, the pair raised over £10,000 for Marie Curie and Macmillan nurses. Sadly, Malcolm lost his own battle with cancer in 2015, and in memory of her friend, in 2016 – her 60th year – Aly ran to the other tip of the country in the inaugural Cape Wrath Ultra. Continuing to inspire everyone she meets with her passion for running and exploration on a magnificent scale, Aly shows no signs of slowing down.

Further information
- *The End to End Trail* by Andy Robinson (Cicerone Press)

Thrilled to be on the home straight (Photo credit: Chris Wren)

*Magnificent Burgos Cathedral
(Photo credit: Richard Lendon)*

ON THE WAY

Running the Camino de Santiago with Richard Lendon

In his head torch beam Richard could see his own breath. Above him, stars twinkled in the purple-blue sky. Outside the doorway of the *albergue* – pilgrim hostel – two bleary-eyed pilgrims pulled on their packs, greeting him with, '*Hola, buen Camino!*' At 6am it was too early for a hostel breakfast, so he munched on a *bocadillo* as he walked – a cheese and chorizo sandwich, bought the previous afternoon. At the edge of the village he started to run, glad to warm up, and soon a crimson sunrise started to streak the sky. Somewhere, a dog was barking and roosters began their wake-up call.

It was May 2015 and Richard Lendon, a Cumbria-based GP, was running the Camino de Santiago to mark his 50th birthday. A keen ultra-runner, he'd considered the usual long-distance challenges, like the Pennine Way and Bob Graham, but was inspired by a film called *The Way* – the story of a father who, in grief and as homage to his dead son, decides to walk the pilgrimage route carrying his ashes.

'The Camino was a pilgrimage for me,' explains Richard. 'My vicar says running is my form of prayer and I think he's right. Running 500 miles was also a present to myself for my 50th. I was hunting for something special. Obviously there was the physical challenge of the distance, but I was doing it for spiritual reasons.'

Over 100,000 people make the 500-mile journey every year, most taking 5–6 weeks. With no fixed schedule and only the first and last night's accommodation booked, Richard planned for 16 days, covering over 30 miles a day – a challenge even for someone who has run the Marathon des Sables, UTMB and Spine.

'I think I enjoy my own running adventures more than races. I'll often go off for a couple of days near home, stopping over wherever my fancy takes me. I love the freedom. It's so therapeutic, especially if you don't see anyone for hours. It's good for the soul.'

From the Pyrenean foothills, the Camino crosses the undulating *meseta* – 150 miles of plains on the central plateau of Spain. Some walkers bus through there, believing it's dull, but Richard loved winding through the sparsely populated countryside, passing through villages suspended in time, Rioja vineyards, acres of rippling green wheat and cornfields laced with poppies. Many of the hills are crowned with the ruins of *castillos* and he was constantly accompanied by birdsong, often cuckoos now so rare back home.

Lunch time on Day 1 – 26km done, a few to go! (Photo credit: Richard Lendon)

Because he ran three walking stages each day, he was usually alone for the first couple of hours before passing groups of walkers bunched up on the trail who'd started from villages ahead. One morning, passing two women, one of them asked, 'Are you the English doctor running the Camino?' He stopped to chat, surprised that his reputation had preceded him. 'Running a marathon every day can't be good for you!' said the other. Richard smiled, resisting the temptation to say, 'Actually, it's an ultra-marathon!'

The walkers usually stopped by 3pm, so he had the afternoon trails to himself before looking for a place to stay. One evening he stayed in the sleepy village of Hornillos del Camino, in its hostel in the main square, next to the church. At 6pm he was sitting in the sun, writing his journal and sipping a beer. He'd already showered, rinsed his gear and had his pilgrim record card stamped. That night's bed would be a bunk in a huge dormitory.

'The *albergues* were part of the experience,' he says. 'Nights in your own room are less fun. It's that community thing. I learnt there's more to life than bricks and mortar. The dingiest hostels could be the best evenings. It was all about the people and the ambience.'

That evening he ate dinner with an Irish woman and an American brother and sister who kept calling him 'sir', despite being well into their 60s. Every day he added to his Camino country list, meeting pilgrims from Brazil to Korea. On the trails the youngest he encountered was a Spanish toddler being pushed in a buggy by his mum. 'People told me I was an inspiration as I ran past them. I always made a point of stopping because I knew I wasn't. I'd be home, finished and in my own bed and they would still be walking. People who walk day after day for five weeks are the real inspiration.'

Richard loved the pattern of his days. 'Life is simple on the Camino,' he says. 'Get up, run and walk, rest, sleep, interspersed with eating. For me, the best thing about multi-day running is escapism. And it's amazing how little you need – just what's on your back. It's a good life lesson really.'

It was 10am, just outside Viana, and Richard was hungry again after an early breakfast. A brightly coloured *donativo* stall enticed him with snacks, fruit, drinks and fresh sugared doughnuts. The stallholder couldn't change his €20 note but insisted he take something because he was a *peregrino* (pilgrim).

It seemed Richard was constantly famished, sometimes waking in the night to rummage for food, trying not to disturb other guests. His lunchtime *bocadillo* would often be wolfed down mid-morning, followed by coffee and cake later. 'I stopped lots for emergency food,' he laughs. 'Ice cream, pastries, chocolate, sweets and cans of coke. The five main food groups!'

Richard's refreshments took an unusual turn one morning at Irache Monastery, in an area renowned for its wine and other produce. 'I sampled the red from the famous wine fountain on the wall opposite the monastery; it was only 7.30am but it would have been rude not to! I promptly missed a turning though. Perhaps a bit early to be drinking!'

Richard always stopped at churches and monasteries along the way. His journey was a moving meditation, with the companionship of fellow pilgrims interspersed with time for reflection. He especially enjoyed the peaceful hostels run by nuns and the special pilgrim masses. 'The priest in Santiago said the Camino is about three things: time alone, time with others and time with God. The third is obvious, but the first two are interesting and also true.'

After 10 days he developed blisters on his feet and had to stifle a laugh when a walker recommended that a ballooning blister on his toe should been seen by a doctor. He was also suffering sore Achilles and calf muscles from the hard-packed trails and at times, through his pain, it felt like an invisible energy was pulling him along. 'I was very aware of the 1500 years of footsteps on the Camino before me. Other people noticed this feeling too. It was very strange.'

On day 12 his spirits reached rock bottom. 'It was my last full day and it was grim, with 50 miles to go. My calves were destroyed. It was miserable and cold. I dropped a glove and had to go back for it. I could barely walk. Even chocolate and ice cream didn't help! In a church I burst into tears, but back on the trail I met some Irish guys who cheered me up. Somehow I did 35 miles, but I only ran two of them.

'Then there was a moment that afternoon,' he adds, 'in a glade with flowers and birds. It felt like I could see every colour and hear every sound. It lasted 20 or 30 seconds. It was like some kind of altered awareness and one of the most spiritual

A typical albergue or pilgrim hostel (Photo credit: Richard Lendon)

Colourful signage on the Camino (Photo credit: Richard Lendon)

moments of my life. So, my lowest point and highest point were on the same day. It's often that way with races too. My favourite part is always a moment – like when the light shines a certain way, or when you see or hear something.'

With mixed emotions, he reached the cathedral at Santiago early on his 13th morning. 'It was all a bit underwhelming,' he recalls. 'Lots of noise, too many people. I then understood it was the journey that mattered. The sights, the people, those moments of utter bliss and understanding. The birdsong.'

Richard beat his schedule by four days, averaging over 40 miles a day, but he says, 'It was never about the time, distance or numbers. The Camino de Santiago is a pilgrimage and it was very much that for me. I had many special experiences, encounters and conversations, moments of sheer wonder. It was a remarkable experience – one I'll cherish for the rest of my life.'

Further information
- Richard's blog: richrunnings.blogspot.co.uk
- *The Way of St James* by Alison Raju (Cicerone Press)
- Confraternity of St James: www.csj.org.uk

Stanton Reservoir, 10 miles from Chipping Campden (Photo credit: Kev Reynolds)

SEVEN GO RUNNING

Four days on the Cotswold Way with Lily Dyu and friends

'Anyone want a banana?' Pete pointed to the crate of fruit that was spilling onto the floor of the minibus.

'Or how about a feta and courgette muffin?' said Jim, standing outside the van, uncovering a tray. Ten heads immediately swung around. We'd been pulling snacks out of bags – pretzels, gels, bars and chocolate – and getting 'five a day' hadn't seemed a priority.

It was a sunny Saturday lunchtime in August 2013, our second of four days running the Cotswold Way. A couple of months earlier I had mentioned to my friend Pete Mainstone that I was thinking of fastpacking the route, which passes near his home, and staying at guesthouses. 'Don't do that,' he said, 'you can stay at mine! And I'll see if anyone else wants to do it and if someone will drive.'

That's how I found myself with a dozen members of Thornbury Running Club, eating freshly baked muffins after a morning's run through glorious English countryside. That day's support driver was Ray Sunnucks, the club physiotherapist, who was being creative with Kinesio tape, stretching wild, fluorescent ribbons across another runner's calves.

Jim Williams was one of seven – along with myself, Pete, Nancy Harding, Judy Mills, Jo Plumbley and Nick Langridge – who were running the whole thing, while others were joining for individual days or sections. Jim was a keen allotment owner and a foodie. The day before, we'd watched enviously as he ate curry and flatbreads for lunch and later pulled out a cheese sandwich on homemade sourdough. Bored with our own provisions, we were fascinated to see what he would unwrap at each rendezvous.

The Cotswold Way is 102 miles long and largely follows a limestone escarpment, from Chipping Campden to Bath. During our run we covered roughly a marathon each day, with a Munro's worth of climbing, up to viewpoints looking out to the Malverns and Brecon Beacons, and dropping to honey-stoned villages and weaving through ancient beech woodland. We also passed historic sites, like the burial mound of Belas Knap and Sudeley Castle, where Jim – an archaeologist at English Heritage as well as a gastronome – provided us with a guided commentary.

That second afternoon, after a stiff climb, we stopped on top of Cooper's Hill, of cheese-rolling fame. Our gaze was drawn away from the fantastic westward views as we imagined people throwing themselves down the vertiginous, grassy hillside, chasing a wheel of cheddar. Even the keen fell runners in the group shook their heads in awe and disbelief. We continued on shady forest paths, dropping to and climbing out of lush valleys until, an hour earlier than expected, we suddenly came across Ray

Judy weaving through summer fields

and the minibus, parked on a steep, narrow lane. He'd forgotten that he was teaching a spinning class that evening and needed to get home, thus cutting our day short by three miles.

'Just can't get the staff these days!' joked Pete, as we piled into the minibus. He looked at the untouched box of fruit. 'Anyone want a banana?'

Pete is somewhat expert at arranging these trips. Over the past 20 years, the retired police officer has raised over £60,000 for the cancer charity CLIC Sargent by organising relay runs, including: Land's End to John O'Groats and back; running from Thornbury to its twinned town of Bockenem in Germany; a relay to Budapest to visit a CLIC centre the runners had helped to fund; not to mention many of the UK's long-distance paths. He and friends also took part in a record-breaking run across Russia, from Vladivostok to St Petersburg.

'I'm so lucky to have seen so much of the world and to have made so many friends – all through running,' says Pete. 'I feel so privileged. But the best things from those trips were the people and seeing the impact that our fundraising made.'

On our third day, new members joined us and seemed to enjoy what was effectively a long fartlek session, looping back repeatedly to those of us with heavy legs as we trotted through hay meadows and rippling fields of golden wheat. Up on the Cotswold escarpment, we regrouped to admire the views of the surrounding countryside and down to the Severn Estuary, beneath blue skies and drifting clouds. Nick was quick to point out to Pete, a proud Welshman, that Wales was, on the other hand, obscured by grey mist.

For Judy, who has taken part in several of Pete's running adventures, it's the sense of a journey that she enjoys: 'They're really fun trips as we're never worried about finishing, just having a few days of running, eating and laughing. But I also love that we're always moving on. I don't want to keep going back to the start after each run. It's a bit like life. And even if I do go back to the same place, it's changed or I've changed. It can never be the same and I don't want it to be.'

It was a hot day, and by lunchtime some people wanted to change their clothes. After enjoying that day's lunch – a beautiful home-made pasta salad – Jim had erected his daughter's pink pop-up tent and was changing inside, to much teasing. Several of us crowded around Nick, who was wearing a Cotswold Way Relay event t-shirt with the route profile emblazoned across the front. As we traced the bumps and spikes, to plot our progress south, he didn't seem unhappy to have four women admiring his chest.

Later that afternoon, our luck ran out with the weather and we were caught in thundery showers as we ran along fields to our finish at Hawkesbury Upton. Ray and

On the final miles towards Bath
(Photo credit: Judy Mills)

his spinning class were quickly blamed for this misfortune, having added the extra miles to the day. Led by Nancy, half the runners then disappeared into the pub while the rest searched the van for snacks and dry clothes. There were still plenty of bananas left.

The last morning was cool and dry and Nick, dressed simply in t-shirt and shorts, waited while some of us pulled on packs and bum-bags. 'What are you all carrying?' he asked, 'We're meeting the minibus in an hour!' He had never run four

100 miles later – seven runners at Bath Abbey (Photo credit: Judy Mills)

marathons in four days, and had so far run every step, including every hill, leading the charge up each climb while most of us walked. 'I was challenged by a friend in Dursley Running Club,' he said, grinning, 'and a run is a run, after all.'

It turned out to be another perfect summer day, and our string of explorers continued south through fields and woods until eventually Bath was laid out below us in the sunshine. An hour later, the pack of Thornbury runners – a flash of red and blue, their club colours – with myself in tow were prowling around Bath city centre among bemused tourists and shoppers, searching for the abbey. There, outside the entrance, stood Pete's daughter and family, along with Jim's dad who had travelled all the way from Sussex to see him finish. Pete tried to introduce me as his new wife; his daughter rolled her eyes and his granddaughters groaned, 'Oh Granddad!' clearly unfazed by his humour.

By coincidence, Pete's son-in-law was the stonemason who had made the plaque marking the end of the Cotswold Way. We assembled around his handiwork for photos at the finish of our 100-mile run. To celebrate that evening, Jo was hosting a barbecue for everyone. At the top of the menu, she told me, would be baked chocolate bananas.

Further information
- *The Cotswold Way* by Kev Reynolds (Cicerone Press)
- www.nationaltrail.co.uk/cotswold-way

Route ideas

Sunset on Loch Hourn. Cut off from the road network, Knoydart is a great place to explore by fastpacking (Route 8) (Photo credit: Chris Councell)

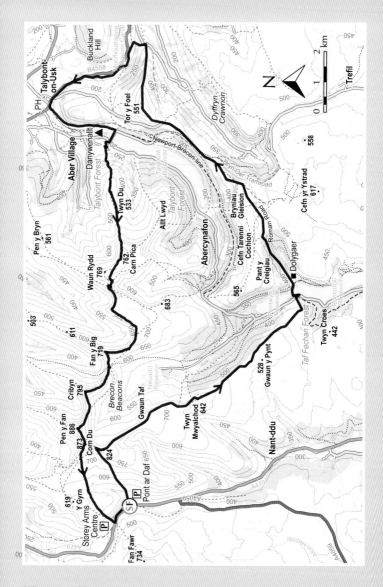

United Kingdom

ROUTE 1
Brecon Beacons

A classic circuit of the highest peaks, escarpments and ridges of South Wales

Start/Finish	Pont ar Daf car park on the A470 near Libanus, Powys
Distance	47km (29 miles)
Total ascent	2050m (6730ft)
Duration	2 days, with an overnight stop in Talybont
Terrain	Good mountain paths (often paved); ridge, moorland and canal paths without especially technical terrain. Route passes through sections of boggy ground. Apart from steep climbs and descents around main summits, a very runnable route.
High point	Pen y Fan, 886m (2907ft)
Navigation	Straightforward in good weather; in poor conditions good navigational skills are needed
Where to stay	Guesthouses, bunkhouse, inns and hostel in Talybont-on-Usk

The Brecon Beacons National Park contains some of the most spectacular and distinctive upland scenery in southern Britain. Much of the area is formed of Old Red Sandstone, resulting in rolling peaks, escarpments and long ridges, making it fantastic trail-running terrain. It is also home to Pen y Fan, the highest mountain in southern Britain at 886m.

This two-day circuit visits the highest peaks of the central Brecon Beacons, as well as the varied surroundings, from secluded reservoirs and forest to gentle pasture and quiet canal. The charming village of Talybont-on-Usk offers plenty of accommodation and pubs for an overnight stop.

The route

A straightforward climb on the main path to Pen y Fan brings you to the long escarpment above **Gwaun Taf**. The route then drops between the **Pontsticill** and **Pentwyn** reservoirs before heading over moorland and above the forested slopes overlooking **Talybont Reservoir**. It's a stiff

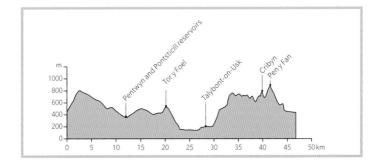

climb over **Tor y Foel** and then a lovely descent through successive pastures takes you onto the canal path to **Talybont village**. On the second day the route climbs back into the mountains and past the giant cairn of **Carn Pica** to join a wonderful escarpment path to the summits of **Fan y Big**, **Cribyn**, **Pen y Fan** and **Corn Du** before returning to the start through a quiet hidden valley.

Highlights

- Pen y Fan and Corn Du, the two highest peaks in South Wales, plus their neighbour, Cribyn
- Superb running on escarpments, ridges and open moorland
- Quiet reservoirs and forests, hidden in the mountains
- The beautiful and peaceful Monmouthshire and Brecon Canal – the most popular visitor attraction in the national park

A delicious descent on the slopes of Tor y Foel with superb views of Sugar Loaf mountain

Just a couple more summits to go – Corn Du and Pen y Fan

- Fantastic views of the whole area, from the Carmarthen Fans in the west to the Black Mountains in the east.

> ### › Did you know?

It's perhaps not as well known as the other classic 'rounds', like the Bob Graham, but the Brecon Beacons Traverse is a long-distance fell-running challenge across the national park. It's a linear route of 118km taking in 31 summits over 610m, with 5000m of ascent. The goal is to complete the route within 24 hours and the fastest known crossing was by Mark Hartell in 1993 in 14 hours 42 minutes.

Top tips
- Carry sufficient water for each day as there is nowhere to fill up en route
- Watch out for deep bogs on the ridges and upland sections
- Pick shoes with good grip on wet rock because of the steep paved paths between summits
- Running poles are helpful but not essential
- Pen y Fan is very popular with walkers, especially at the weekends, so an early start is recommended to ensure a parking space.

Where to find out more
For more on this route, see: https://www.cicerone.co.uk/957

As he checked me in, the youth hostel receptionist gave me a quizzical look. This was unsurprising since I looked like I'd been in a fight in a farmyard and lost. I had bloodied knees, was caked in peaty mud and was giving off a delicate scent of bog.

'Good day on the hills?' he laughed.

'Yes, a couple of minor mishaps, but a fab day,' I grinned.

The weekend had started well – two days of fine weather forecast and an early start so I was climbing Pen y Fan before the car park was full. I reached the col in mist, and leaving the walkers behind I turned away from the distinctive top of South Wales' highest mountain and onto the long ridge of Graig Gwaun Taf, where I could finally break into a run. The haze cleared to reveal shards of blue sky, with the sun illuminating the yellow gorse on red sandstone. I could see the glinting reservoir – my next destination at the foot of the ridge – and tomorrow's mountains to my left. I was soon happily running in the sunshine on a seemingly dry, peaty footpath, taking in views of the Carmarthen Fans.

Suddenly, a split second later, I was chest-deep in a cold, smelly bog. Lost in my thoughts, I hadn't seen the pool of lighter-coloured 'ground' with suspicious green moss quivering on the top. I knew of the notorious bogs in the Peak District and Dartmoor, but not here in the Brecon Beacons. Could bog suck me in like quicksand? Alone, a long way from home, this seemed an embarrassingly stupid way to meet my maker. I then realised I could, of course, doggy paddle, so I splashed and pulled myself out. Mid Wales

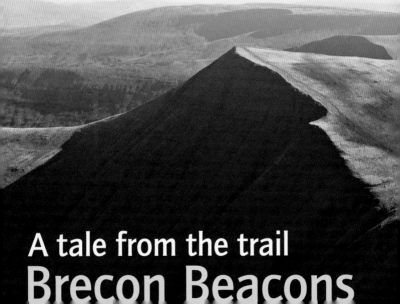

A tale from the trail
Brecon Beacons

is home to the famous bog snorkelling championships, so perhaps my wild swim shouldn't have come as such a surprise.

I spotted a stile into the edge of some forest and crossed into the enclosure and onto drier ground. Luckily it was now warm and sunny. *I'll dry off*, I thought, *but I'll probably frighten any children out with their parents.* Covered in stinking mud, I continued on my way, carefully watching the ground and cursing myself for a silly mistake so soon into my trip.

The trail dropped down to the Pontsticill reservoir and then climbed open moorland on the slopes of Bryniau Gleision. It was here, running and admiring the views, that I tripped on the stony track and landed on my front, winding myself. I was a bit sore but had suffered no major damage as far as I could tell, but now I had scraped knees as well as a coating of dried-out bog. Not a good look.

The rest of that day's run was a joy and thankfully uneventful, passing the Talybont reservoir and forest, climbing Tor y Foel, then dropping onto a deliciously shady canal path to Talybont. I arrived in time for well-deserved tea and cake before heading to the hostel, never more in need of a shower. Over dinner, I chatted to a woman who was working her way through all the youth hostels in England and Wales and had just 'bagged' the Georgian Wilderhope Manor and a castle in Monmouthshire.

The next morning, with my t-shirt still streaked brown despite vigorous handwashing, I ran along the escarpments of the central Beacons. Above me, the cheery skylarks sang as I enjoyed views over much of the national park, its peaks rolling across the landscape like a green, petrified wave. Passing walkers, I took in the summits – Fan y Big, Cribyn, busy Pen y Fan and its table-top neighbour, Corn Du – before dropping down into a hidden valley and returning to Storey Arms.

Travelling back from the Man Versus Horse Marathon the following weekend, I mentioned to a friend that I'd run the race cautiously because my side was still sore from my fall in the Beacons. 'Does it hurt to sneeze or cough?' he asked. It turned out that I'd cracked a rib when I'd landed on my water bottle.

Trail running for me is mostly about enjoying beautiful surroundings, but that weekend I was painfully reminded to always stop to look at the views whenever the terrain also demands your attention!

From Pen y Fan the peaks of Cribyn and Fan y Big look like a petrified wave

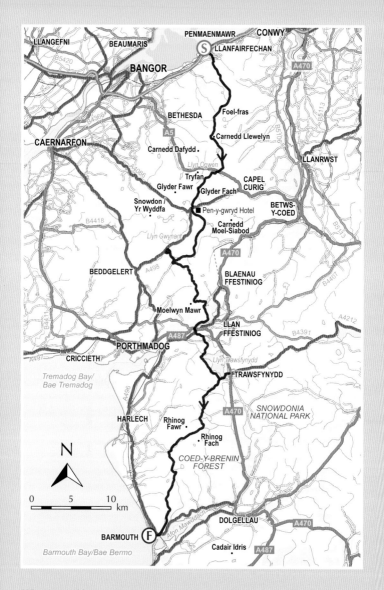

ROUTE 2
Snowdonia

A coast-to-coast journey through Wales' highest mountain ranges

Start	Llanfairfechan
Finish	Barmouth
Distance	99km (62 miles)
Total ascent	4325m (14,190ft)
Duration	4 days
Terrain	Varied, from grassy hillsides, rocky slopes and ridges, and tussocky, boggy moor to technical mountain terrain, with some scrambling required (although this can be avoided by variants). The route is all on footpaths, rather than trackless ground. With steep climbs and rough terrain, this route will generally involve a lot of walking; however, there are sections of great running.
High point	Carnedd Llewelyn, 1064m (3491ft)
Navigation	Route requires the ability to navigate, especially in poor conditions. Paths range from obvious and well marked to faint.
Where to stay	Guesthouses, bunkhouses and hostels en route, although limited choices. Wild camping (with care) is also an option.

This is a challenging but superb crossing of Snowdonia's landscapes of myth and legend – from coast and estuary to craggy mountain ridges and idyllic wooded valleys. It crosses several mountain ranges, each with its own beauty and character, taking you to places rarely visited and surprising you with relics of some of the area's industrial past.

The route is intimate with the mountains but winds its way through them rather than going over the highest summits – although variants allow you to bag the peaks. The days can be long, due to the location of accommodation and the amount of climbing, but this is a fastpacking journey that's well worth all the effort.

Possible overnight options include Helyg in the Ogwen Valley, near Capel Curig (campsite and bunkhouse at Gwern Gof Isaf and Gwern Gof Uchaf), Nantgwynant (youth hostel off-route) and Trawsfynydd.

The route

From Llanfairfechan you cross the Carneddau into the Ogwen Valley, then go over the **Glyder** ridge, passing Tryfan and heading down past the iconic **Pen y Gwryd Hotel** before following the lonely Siabod-Moelwyn ridge to **Nantgwynant**. From here, a traverse of the eerie, quarry-scarred Moelwyns brings you to the verdant Ffestiniog valley, then **Trawsfynydd Lake**. Finally there's a passage of Coed y Brenin Forest and the **Rhinogs** before a lofty ridge, overlooking Cadair Idris and the Mawddach Estuary, leads you to **Barmouth**.

Highlights

- A mountain running adventure through some of the most spectacular and wild ranges of the UK, with the option of taking in the summits
- The diversity of Snowdonia's ranges and landscapes
- The sense of history on a remote, quiet route, little seen by most visitors
- The satisfaction of a coast-to-coast traverse of Snowdonia National Park
- Great running on the whaleback ridge of the Carneddau, through Coed y Brenin, the Rhinogs and the final ridge into Barmouth.

Top tips

- Choose shoes with good tread on wet rock and muddy paths
- Be prepared for quickly changing mountain weather
- The route is not waymarked and you need good map-reading skills
- Be aware there are sections with very indistinct paths
- Accommodation is limited in Helyg and the Ogwen Valley – if staying at one of the bunkhouses, ask if you can leave a sleeping bag and food there (to avoid carrying it) and collect them on your return car journey
- Read the guidebooks carefully if you'd rather avoid sections with scrambling and exposure, which are most likely to be on the high-level variants.

Where to find out more

- This route is taken from *From Snowdonia to the Gower: A Coast-to-Coast Walk across Highest Wales* by John Gillham (Diadem Books; now out of print but available second-hand)

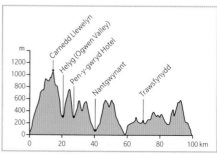

Breathtaking views of Snowdon from the Siabod/Moelwyn ridge

- The Snowdonia Way, from Conwy to Machynlleth, follows a similar route and would make a great fastpacking trip. It has low- and high-level options, in 6–10 stages. See *The Snowdonia Way* by Alex Kendall (Cicerone Press)

- The Cambrian Way is a high-level route from North to South Wales which could also be used for a traverse of Snowdonia. See *Cambrian Way: The Mountain Connoisseur's Walk* by AJ Drake (Cambrian Way Trust).

> Did you know?

This trip gives a taste of the first two stages of the legendary Dragon's Back Race – a five-day journey following the mountainous spine of Wales from north to south, originally based on John Gillham's book. Badged as the toughest five-day mountain race in the world, it was first staged in 1992 as a pairs event, won by Helene Whitaker (née Diamantides) and Martin Stone. The race was next run 20 years later in 2012, when Helene returned to the race, achieving first woman and fourth overall.

It was early on a Saturday morning in September. Mist rose from grassy slopes glistening with dew and two wild ponies nuzzled in the sunshine, a hay scent drifting from their dung as it steamed on the path. Just after Drum, the guidebook's main route dropped left into a valley, avoiding the summits; but seduced by fine weather, I made an impulsive decision to carry on over the Carneddau.

It was barely 8am, so I was shocked to see a walker descending from Foel-Fras. We stopped to talk. He'd spent three days hiking from Nasareth and would finish that day in Conwy. He'd bivvied the previous night, high in the mountains. Since I'd seen a brilliant night sky from the coast, I asked what his view had been like. 'Ah yes. The sky was amazing,' he answered, with a far-away look in his eyes. He seemed to have been enchanted by his night beneath the stars.

My decision to continue on the high route was rewarded with easy running between Foel-Fras, Garnedd Uchaf and Foel Frach; but ahead, Carnedd Llewelyn was now swathed in clag. How quickly things change. With no discernible path, I climbed in mist, on slopes peppered with scree, up to a rocky plateau. Thankfully the cloud cleared to reveal the top – crowned with a giant, rocky cairn dating from the Bronze Age – and views of the surrounding peaks. Below me, I was amazed to see a woman in shorts and vest, running like a gazelle, perhaps recce-ing the Paddy Buckley Round.

I descended to the Penywaun-wen ridge, with Cwm Eigiau on one side and the Ffynnon Llugwy reservoir on the other. Nearing the col, I stopped to watch climbers on the buttresses of Craig yr Ysfa and found myself thinking about 'deep play' – the term coined by philosopher Jeremy Bentham – a game with stakes so high no rational person would play it.

As I continued, the path suddenly disappeared over a protrusion of slabby rock. The guidebook had briefly mentioned that care was needed here, but I hadn't expected this. Having a fear of exposure, I performed an inelegant bum-shuffle, lowering myself slowly down until, with

A tale from the trail
Snowdonia

relief, I rejoined the path. But ahead the ridge narrowed, with a drop either side. My stomach churned as I walked on, never looking down.

A hiker with a dog approached, and beyond him I could see the steep scramble to Pen yr Helgi Du, my objective. The hiker assured me I'd be fine. 'If my dog can manage it, you can!' he said, and then, 'If in doubt, keep left.' As I climbed, like Cheryl Strayed in *Wild* when she was alone on the Pacific Crest Trail, I repeated to myself, 'I am not afraid! I am not afraid!' My heart thumped loudly; I tried to focus on each next step. Eventually I was on the top. The cairn was unimpressive, but I'd never been happier to see an old pile of stones. A delicious descent on a broad, grassy ridge, with wonderful views of Tryfran, dropped me into the Ogwen Valley.

That evening, alone in the bunkhouse kitchen, with clothes drying over chairs and the oven on full blast to warm the room, I was relieved to have survived the day unscathed – and happier than if I'd checked into the Ritz. I was the only person staying and as I cooked my dinner I promised myself I'd stick to the main route for rest of my trip.

Over the next three days this route, despite missing the summits, took me high through hidden places. Quiet paths led past gleaming tarns with unparalleled views of Snowdon, before dropping through a wild valley to Nantgwynant. In perfect solitude I discovered eerie, abandoned slate mines above the Ffestiniog valley, where a train whistled below. Autumn colours tinted the woodland around Trawsfynydd Lake where two disused power stations sat silent on the shore. On my last morning, wind whistled in my ears as I climbed a heather-and-rock-strewn pass in the Rhinogs, before ascending a ridge that would lead me to the coast.

Sitting in Barmouth's harbour with a celebratory bag of chips, watching gulls edge ever closer, I thought about the walker I'd met on that first morning. Perhaps it wasn't a night under the stars that had bewitched him; a journey through the heart of Snowdonia had cast a spell on me too.

Snowdon from a lonely tarn on the Siabod / Moelwyn ridge

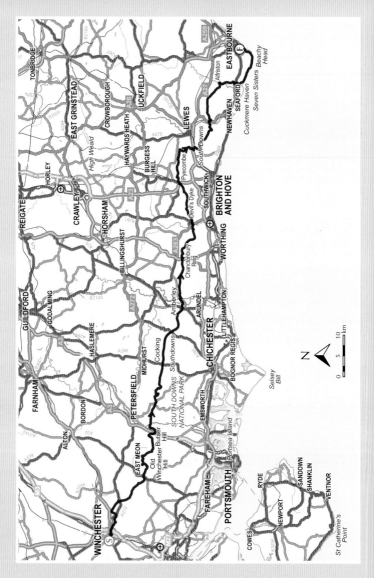

ROUTE 3
South Downs Way

Following the ancient chalk ridgeway from England's Saxon capital to the coast

Start	Winchester
Finish	Eastbourne
Distance	160km (100 miles)
Total ascent	4275m (14,030ft)
Duration	5 or 6 days comfortably, or 4 days (or fewer) of marathon or ultra-distance running
Terrain	Generally easy running on well-made paths and bridleways on rolling chalk downs, through woodland, fields and cliff-top paths.
High point	Butser Hill, 270m (886ft)
Navigation	Easy even in poor weather. Route is fully waymarked.
Where to stay	Hotels, B&Bs, guesthouses, youth hostels, camping barns and campsites en route. Wild camping is not really an option.

The distinctive chalk escarpment of the South Downs – often described as the spine of the South Downs National Park – was formed millions of years ago under a shallow tropical sea. Today, the area is known for its rolling hills, heath and farmland, river valleys, ancient woodland, pretty villages and iconic white cliffs.

The crests of the Downs were used centuries ago as highways above the then-dense forest and mire of the Weald. Today the South Downs Way follows the old routes and drovers' ways on the high chalk ridge through the national park, from England's Saxon capital at Winchester to the dramatic Seven Sisters and Eastbourne on the coast.

With easy terrain, inspiring views and its sense of space and tranquillity, running this route provides an opportunity 'to get away from it all' without having to travel too far in this otherwise busy part of England.

For a full six-day itinerary, East Meon, Cocking, Amberley, Pyecombe and Alfriston would make convenient overnight stops.

The view along the Fulking escarpment, near the Devil's Dyke, stretches far into the Sussex Weald (Photo credit: Kev Reynolds)

The route

From Winchester the route leads through rolling farmland then up onto the Downs, past **Old Winchester Hill** and the high point of **Butser Hill**, dropping briefly around South Harting before regaining the escarpment. It then follows a mix of woodland and open spaces along the escarpment's northern edge, passing the **Amberley Wild Brooks** and continuing onto **Chanctonbury Ring** and the dramatic dry valley at the Devil's Dyke before leading down to **Pyecombe**. Views stretch to the Channel as the Way curves down to the coast, through Cuckmere Nature Reserve and then onto the roller-coaster cliff-top path over the **Seven Sisters** and **Beachy Head**, with a final steep descent to **Eastbourne**.

Highlights

- Excellent underfoot conditions and easy running over gently rolling chalk downland and ridges
- Visible ancient history along the route, plus pretty villages and fine pubs
- Superb, expansive views – north over the Weald and down to the coast, plus the drama of the Seven Sisters at Sussex
- Good variety of scenery, from rolling farmland and woodland to estuary and cliff paths
- Fully waymarked, with many bridleway paths and few stiles
- An ideal route for those new to fastpacking
- Good access to the route by public transport, so it can easily be split into shorter trips.

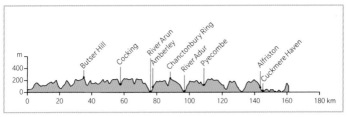

Top tips

- You can use baggage transfer services on this route
- Run from west to east so the wind is on your back and you finish with the Seven Sisters and the sea
- The route largely stays high and infrequently visits towns and villages. While you pass teashops and occasional pubs, it's best to carry snacks and enough water for each day
- After rain, chalk tracks soon become slippery, which can cause problems on steep descents. Be aware of this when selecting footwear
- For long periods you may be fully exposed to the elements with little shelter or shade. Be prepared for all conditions.

The most westerly of the Seven Sisters (Photo credit: Kev Reynolds)

Where to find out more

- *The South Downs Way* by Kev Reynolds (Cicerone Press)
- www.nationaltrail.co.uk/ south-downs-way
- Contour Trail Running Holidays offer this route as a supported, self-guided trip www.contoursrun.co.uk

> ## Did you know?

Each summer, the Oxfam Trailwalker sees teams running or walking 100km through the rolling countryside of the South Downs in under 30 hours. The event in fact started its life as a training exercise for the Gurkhas in the rugged mountains of Hong Kong's New Territories. Run on the 100km MacLehose Trail, it grew into an annual Oxfam Hong Kong fundraising challenge and in 1997, with the return of the colony to China, the Gurkha Regiment was relocated to Southeast England, bringing with them their long-distance challenge.

I'd wanted to visit Chanctonbury Ring ever since I'd read about it in Robert Macfarlane's *The Old Ways*. The place is said to be haunted and without knowing this, Macfarlane spent a night sleeping beneath the trees only to be woken at 2am by the sound of screaming above him. Eventually the terrifying noise stopped and although he now believes it may have been tawny owls, he doesn't seem entirely convinced.

The Ring is a hill on the Sussex Downs at over 200m above sea level, and until the great storm of 1987 it was crowned with magnificent beech trees, many of which were destroyed. It lies on the South Downs Way and used to be the halfway point when the route stretched from Eastbourne to Buriton. I was running the Way in the unseasonably warm autumn of 2014.

By coincidence, it was Halloween the morning I reached the Ring. Hours earlier, I'd crept out of a guesthouse in Amberley, skipping their cooked breakfast in exchange for a generous packed lunch that was weighing down my pack. At 7am,

the darkness hid the beautiful thatched cottages and castle that had greeted me the previous afternoon, when I'd watched red deer, swans and cattle clustered on the Amberley Wild Brooks – acres of marshland and water meadows threaded by the River Arun. Now, in the woods, owls called out as dawn began to bleach the sky.

You can see the clump of trees for miles before you reach it. I ran towards the hilltop, passing sheep as they grazed in the morning sunshine. To the south I could make out the hazy coast and glinting buildings of Brighton, while the vast patchwork of fields, woodland and meadows of the Weald stretched to the north. As I bounded up the hillside I was suddenly seized by a strange breathlessness – a feeling of being weighed down. This was odd, as the track wasn't steep. The feeling lasted maybe 20 seconds and then passed. Around me, everything was normal – just sheep, grass and sunshine. Were my mind and body playing tricks on me? My heart was thumping wildly as I reached the top.

Legend has it that Satan dug the Devil's Dyke to flood the churches of the Weald

The Ring is now a bedraggled circle of beech replanted in the centre, and around it an ancient earth ditch. The place had been the site of an Iron Age hill fort, then later a Roman temple. With wind rustling the shadowy treetops, I was glad I wasn't staying there overnight. Legend has it that you can raise the Devil by running around the trees seven times in an anti-clockwise direction. When he appears, he will offer you a bowl of soup in exchange for your soul. I didn't have the energy for a hilltop training session and my packed lunch had to be eaten anyhow, so forgoing the chance of hot food, I headed downhill as two dog-walkers approached from below and gave me a cheery 'Good morning'.

It seemed the Devil had been busy in these parts. I stopped to eat my sandwiches at the Devil's Dyke, a dramatic, deep dry valley and the largest single coombe of chalk karst in Britain. Local legend says it was dug by the Devil so that the sea would flood the churches of the Weald. The dyke resembles a huge crack in the earth and that day the paths plunging into its depths were busy with walkers enjoying the autumn sunshine.

It was easy, flowing running over the gently rolling chalk downs, passing burial mounds and other historic sites, and after a leisurely 22 miles I reached the tiny village of Pyecombe mid-afternoon. I was drawn to its flint and pebbledash Norman church where a sign invited walkers into a side-room where you could help yourself to the kettle and biscuits in exchange for a donation. Soon I was sat outside on a bench, drinking tea and watching autumn leaves drift down to the ground.

A black cat appeared and started to circle around me, sniffing my rucksack for food. I probably looked a frightening mess in my running gear, but I had no plans to go trick-or-treating that evening. I'd had plenty of Halloween fun already, so I was ready for a bowl of hot soup – but in the spook-free comfort of the local pub.

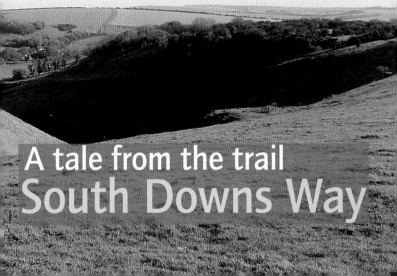

A tale from the trail
South Downs Way

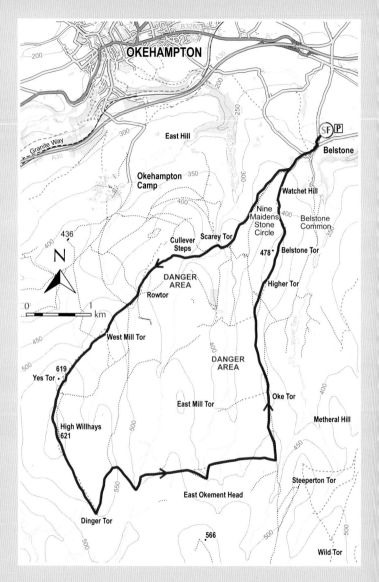

ROUTE 4
Dartmoor

Touring the Tors on a wild camping adventure

Start/Finish	Belstone
Distance	15km (9 miles)
Total ascent	380m (1240ft)
Duration	24 hours (2 half-days)
Terrain	Very runnable route on good paths over ridges; includes moorland with boggy areas, some areas of granite clitter (care needed here), a small trackless section over marshy ground, and unmetalled vehicle tracks.
High point	High Willhays, 621m (2037ft)
Navigation	Easy in good conditions; navigational skills required in poor weather.
Where to stay	Wild camping

Often described as 'the last wilderness in England', Dartmoor's landscape is quite unlike any other: rolling hills topped with strangely sculpted granite tors; heather-clad moors; wetlands; and deep wooded valleys with fast-flowing rivers. It is also one of the richest areas in the world for prehistoric archaeology: the moor is studded with evidence of the Bronze Age with hut circles, standing stones, stone circles, stone rows and burial kists (chambers). The national park (sections of it, anyway – see www.dartmoor.gov.uk for a map of exactly where) is the only place in England where you can legally wild camp.

Of all the places on Dartmoor, perhaps the northern area of the Okehampton Range feels the most wild and untouched, since it is uninhabited and used by the MOD for training exercises. This run takes in those dramatic landscapes with a relatively short, exhilarating circuit and an overnight wild camp.

Between Dinger Tor and Oke Tor the route passes close to several streams, offering a choice of camping spots.

The rugged wilderness of northern Dartmoor

The route

From Belstone a short section of the Tarka Trail leads you to **Scarey Tor** then past the **Cullever Steps** (stepping-stones) up to **Rowtor**, which is followed by **West Mill Tor**. From here it's a short descent then climb to **Yes Tor**; onto to **High Willhays**; and a trackless section to **Dinger Tor** before joining good tracks through the valley around the head of the East Okemont river. From there the route climbs towards Steeperton Tor, turning off onto a ridge that runs over **Oke Tor**, **Higher Tor** and **Belstone Tor**, before dropping over Belstone Common and back to the start.

Highlights

- A wild camping micro-adventure that can be squeezed into 24 hours or less
- Great running using good tracks and paths between tors, with fantastic ridge sections
- The two highest points in Southern England, Yes Tor and High Willhays
- Wonderful, wild and remote scenery of rugged tors and quiet wooded valleys
- Expansive views over Dartmoor

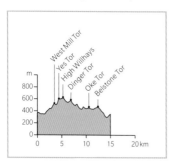

- Visible archaeology including the Nine Maidens stone circle
- Superb night skies over the national park

Top tips
- This run is within the Okehampton Range, which is used by the British Army for exercises. Red flags are raised around the perimeter when live firing is due to take place. You should always check dates for safe access (see below). On most weekends and over the summer it is generally accessible to the public
- If you see any unexploded ordnance or other military debris, do not touch it. Note its location and inform the police
- Wild camping is permitted on much of Dartmoor, but you should check your chosen location (see below)
- Although paths may not be marked, you will find they do exist between many of the tors
- Although not mountainous, running on Dartmoor can be slower than expected and has its own hazards:

watch out for boggy areas, peat hags, heather and ankle-turning tussocky grass
- Care should be taken when running around the tors since there are large areas of boulders and stones strewn on the slopes (clitter).

Where to find out more
- For more on this route, see: https://www.cicerone.co.uk/957
- Another great multi-day run across Dartmoor is the Two Moors Way. See *The Two Moors Way, Devon's Coast to Coast* by Sue Viccars (Cicerone Press)
- MOD live firing times on Dartmoor can be found at www.gov.uk (search 'Dartmoor firing times')
- Permitted wild camping locations can be found at www.dartmoor.gov.uk

'Wow – did you see that one?'

Shooting stars streaked across the night sky, one-a-minute. Some left smoky trails while others flashed hints of green, blue and red as their minerals burned up in the atmosphere. It was better than any firework display I'd ever seen.

The air was chilly and we could see our breath. Outside our tent, a nearly-full moon lit up the moor and stream. Beneath us, we could feel the lumpy pitch through our camping mats. We were fully dressed inside our sleeping bags, with beanies on our heads, faces poking out of the tent to watch the celestial show.

It was midnight on a Saturday in August and we were wild camping on Dartmoor, to see the Perseids meteor shower. We had run in late that afternoon from Belstone, a pretty village above a wooded cleave, having planned to make a circuit of northern Dartmoor over the wild land usually used for military training. In the car park, a local woman told us that the moor was a special place: 'I like to think of it as a favourite uncle. You need to listen to him carefully. And if you're lucky, he might surprise you with gifts.' Her words made me think of the myth of Old Crockern, the spirit of Dartmoor who is said to take care of the land here.

Heading onto the moor beneath overcast skies and into a cool wind, we passed dog-walkers returning to their cars and soon had the place to ourselves. The views stretched to all sides, taking in hilltops crowned with tumbling tors and strewn with worn clitter. There were few trees and the bleached land was spotted in places with the purple and yellow of heather and gorse. This was an elemental landscape of rock and sky,

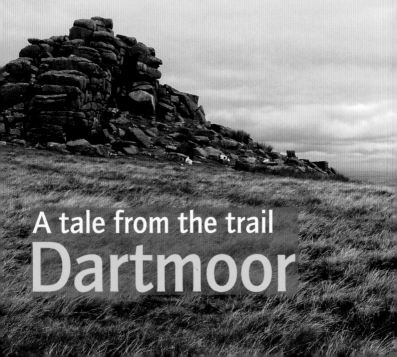

A tale from the trail
Dartmoor

yet the army presence was clear as we passed old lookout buildings, masts and the occasional rifle shell glinting on the ground.

We ran up to Yes Tor, with its Bronze Age burial cairn, and then onto High Willhays, an unremarkable outcrop but at 621m the highest point in southern Britain other than the Brecon Beacons. From there it was a fun descent, winding through marshy ground to Dinger Tor, passing grazing ponies and cattle. An old track led us into the middle of the valley, avoiding the worst of the ankle-turning tussocky grass, as cloudy skies loosened to blue and the sun broke through.

As the sun set, the ring of hills and tors glowed with a golden light and we set up camp in a grassy hollow next to the fledgling East Okement river. After a paddle, we cooked dinner to the sound of the stream, while overhead the sky darkened to a denim-blue, pricked with stars. That night we watched meteors raining overhead until our eyes could stay open no longer and sleep settled over our hidden corner of the moor.

The next morning it was damp and cold and we woke in mist. We ate porridge and cradled tea, sitting on dewy grass as the haze started to lift. By the time we were climbing our first hill, the sun was breaking through. Soon we were enjoying a delicious run along a ridge – a chain of granite outcrops creating a silvery spine on the landscape. With a lot of clitter around, we had to watch the ground as well as enjoying the glorious views of the hills we'd covered the previous day. Finally we reached Belstone Tor with its logan stone, a huge rock balancing on those beneath, and from there we ran down, passing the Nine Maidens – a stone circle where legend has it that a group of women were turned to rock as punishment for dancing on a Sunday and are now fated to dance at noon every day for eternity.

It was well before noon when we wandered back into the village, but the Tors Inn was already open. Coffee and cake were in order to celebrate our Perseids wild camping adventure. We had only paid a short visit to Dartmoor but Old Crockern had been more than generous.

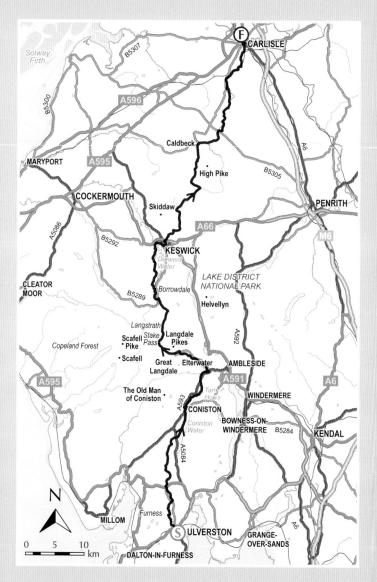

ROUTE 5
Cumbria Way

Traversing the heart of the beautiful Lake District

Start	Ulverston
Finish	Carlisle
Distance	118km (73 miles)
Total ascent	2900m (9510ft)
Duration	4 days comfortably, or 3 days of marathon-distance running
Terrain	Good paths through fields, on fells and lakeside; long sections of hard-packed trails and rocky, rough riverside paths. Most of the route can be run but there is rocky terrain around Stake Pass and a rocky path through the Langstrath valley.
High point	High Pike, 658m (2159ft)
Navigation	Navigational skills are needed, although the route is waymarked in places.
Where to stay	Hotels, B&Bs, guesthouses, youth hostels, camping barns and campsites en route. Wild camping is not really an option.

Ever since the Romantic poets arrived in the 19th century, the Lakeland landscape of craggy mountains, hidden tarns and glittering lakes has been stirring the imaginations of visitors, writers and artists. The area, along with the neighbouring Yorkshire Dales, was the also the birthplace of fell running, through the 19th-century 'guide races' with short, steep up-and-down courses that tested the abilities of the men who guided tourists onto the fells and mountains.

The Cumbria Way crosses through the Lakes, visiting Coniston, the Langdale valley and Keswick, and the passes and valleys that link them. No less enjoyable are some of the less frequented areas at each end of the journey. The official route follows mainly low-level valley paths but is surrounded by magnificent mountains. Without any technical terrain, it is a fantastic way for runners to enjoy the excellent trails and scenery. There are route options to take in the summits if tempted, and for a full three-day itinerary, possible stopovers include Elterwater, Keswick and Carlisle.

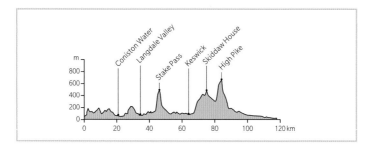

The route

From Ulverston, rolling hills and fields lead you onto the fells of Coniston and along the shore of **Coniston Water**. Here the Cumbria Way heads into the heart of the Lakes, past **Tarn Hows**, through the Langdale valley and over **Stake Pass** before descending through the wild, uninhabited Langstrath valley and through **Borrowdale** to **Derwent Water** and **Keswick**. The route continues to **Caldbeck** over the fells around **Skiddaw** and then over **High Pike**, before following the River Caldew to **Carlisle**.

Highlights

- The satisfaction of crossing Cumbria and Lakeland, from coast to Carlisle
- The grand finale of finishing at Carlisle's Cathedral Quarter
- The sheer variety of Lakeland scenery including rolling farmland, remote valleys and mountain passes, wooded lakesides, dramatic fells and gentle riverside paths
- Quiet, remote, lesser-known sections of the route, especially from Keswick to Carlisle and over High Pike

Enjoying some flat trails on the shores of Coniston Water

> ## Did you know?

Up until 2016 only three people had completed a double Bob Graham Round: Boyd Millen (1977), Roger Baumeister (1979) and Eric Draper (1995). In May 2016 Nicky Spinks became the fourth and fastest in 45 hours and 30 minutes, taking an hour off the previous record set by Roger. Wanting to inspire others and also to raise money for charity, her achievement marked 10 years since a cancer diagnosis. A standard Bob Graham Round involves a 66-mile circuit of 42 Lakeland summits including 27,000ft of elevation gain, to be completed in less than 24 hours. Nicky did all that twice, and became only the second person after Roger – and the first woman – to go sub-48 hours. After finishing, despite suggestions that she go around again, she celebrated with curry and chips.

- Excellent underfoot conditions and great running
- The opportunity to stay at Skiddaw House, one of England's most remote youth hostels
- The option to extend the trip and include mountain variants, such as Coniston Old Man, the Langdale Pikes and Blencathra.

Top tips
- You can use baggage transfer services on this route
- Be prepared for quickly changing mountain weather – although largely low-level, the route includes Stake Pass and the summit of High Pike
- A lot of the trails are hard-packed so choose trail shoes with good cushioning or add cushioned insoles
- The route involves fording streams that may be in spate, so shoes with good tread and running poles are helpful here

- Stone stiles are common in Cumbria and can be slippery in running shoes
- The route can be attempted all year round, depending on accommodation, although snow and ice could make Stake Pass and the traverse over the Back o' Skiddaw more difficult
- Follow the route from south to north and you should have the sun and wind on your back
- The official route can be combined with mountain variants that, if followed, in total only add about 5km (3 miles) to the overall distance.

Where to find out more
- *The Cumbria Way* by John Gillham (Cicerone Press) has both the official route, plus mountain variants
- Contour Trail Running Holidays offers this route as a supported, self-guided trip: www.contoursrun.co.uk

'I've locked the screen on my Garmin,' I groaned.

'Ooh, shall I pray for that as well?' asked the woman, looking up from watering some flowers.

It was early on a Friday morning in July and my friend, Michelle, and I were stood at the sculpture in Ulverston, at the start of the Cumbria Way. A woman in a red fleece, carrying a watering can, had appeared at our side as we studied the map. She was tending the flower tubs in the square and was interested in our plans. As we'd started to leave, she'd stopped us and insisted on saying a prayer for us. Taken aback and slightly embarrassed, we let her carry on. We were running the route over three days, with overnight stops at Elterwater and Keswick and a 30-mile day at the end – perhaps she thought we needed extra help!

Before we left, I managed to unlock the Garmin – through a quick Google search on my phone, rather than divine intervention! I wondered if that woman saw off every Cumbria Way walker, suddenly remembering the start of the Himalayan stage race I'd done, where a village priest had blessed every runner, marking red dots on our foreheads and wrapping ceremonial scarves around our necks.

That afternoon, after miles of rolling farmland, Lakeland-proper started small with Beacon Tarn – a lake in miniature – from where we dropped to Coniston Water. After fording several in-spate streams, Michelle yelled, 'You didn't tell me I'd get wet feet on this trip!' as her

A tale from the trail
Cumbria Way

Gore-Tex trail shoes filled like buckets. A keen runner, this was her first fastpacking trip. Perhaps I hadn't been clear enough that moving 'fast and light' didn't mean acquiring the power to walk on water!

Going light also means not filling your pack with shopping en route. Before starting, we'd spent an hour in our guesthouse ditching socks and spare layers. In Keswick, on the second afternoon, Michelle ran ahead as I lingered at Derwent Water to take photos. After a day with no navigation errors, winding our way from Elterwater over eerie Stake Pass and through the wild Langstrath valley, it took over half an hour to find her among the outdoor shops and holidaymakers. Thankfully, she hadn't bought any new gear or souvenirs!

We left the crowds behind the next morning to reach Skiddaw House, England's highest and one of its most remote youth hostels. Here, we pulled on waterproofs as rain showers darkened the peaks ahead. Crossing the infant River Caldew, we followed boggy paths into the wild, empty valley below the heathered slopes of Great Calva. The rain stopped as we climbed past slag heaps and the abandoned buildings of Carrock mine then up a rough beck-side path to Great Lingy Hill.

From here it was an easy climb to High Pike, the highest point on the Cumbria Way. Looking north, it seemed we would literally fall off the end of the Lakeland fells. There were no more big hills left in England – only low ridges and miles of pastureland between us and Carlisle in the distance. We flew down a long, fun, grassy hillside towards the village below, confidently following a well-worn trail. Unfortunately, we'd picked the wrong route off the top, and reached some abandoned quarries before realising our error.

Having added an extra hour onto what was already our biggest day, our lunchbreak in Caldbeck was more of a mid-afternoon tea-stop and excuse for cake. Replenished, we trotted through quiet woodland before meeting the River Caldew again, whose course we followed to Carlisle through green meadows and fields of rippling wheat, passing ecclesiastical castles and beautiful bridges built in the distinctive, local pink sandstone. From the village of Dalston we joined a cycle path and it was here the heavens opened, with biblical rain bouncing off the tarmac as we approached Carlisle's outskirts.

As we reached the Cathedral Quarter the raindrops were suddenly lit with sunshine as the grey sky split into blue and a rainbow arched overhead. Being soaked didn't dampen our joy at finishing, and from inside the cathedral we could hear an organ and a choir singing. *If the woman from Ulverston could see us now*, I thought, *I'm sure she'd be smiling.*

ROUTE 6
Coast to Coast

Running the breadth of England through three national parks

Start	St Bees
Finish	Robin Hood's Bay
Distance	302km (188 miles)
Total ascent	8880m (29,140ft)
Duration	10 days comfortably, or 7 days of marathon-distance running
Terrain	Footpaths, tracks and minor roads on varied terrain – mountain passes, hills, valleys, farmland, moorland, riverside and coastal paths. Valleys and arable land provide straightforward running, but the hills – particularly in the Lakes – are high and sometimes steep, with rocky footpaths.
High point	Kidsty Pike, 780m (2560ft)
Navigation	Good navigational skills needed – this route is not waymarked
Where to stay	Hotels, B&Bs, guesthouses, youth hostels, camping barns and campsites en route. Wild camping is not really an option.

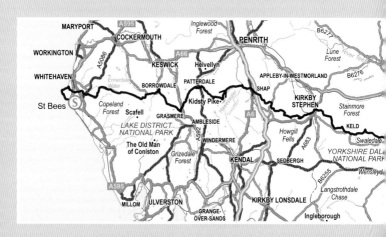

Devising the Coast to Coast walk was a labour of love for Alfred Wainwright, who wrote and illustrated many books about his beloved Lake District. First published in 1973, the route starts at St Bees Head on the Irish Sea and passes through three national parks in the North of England before finishing at Robin Hood's Bay. It's a journey of contrasts, with the grand fells of the Lake District; the beautiful valleys of the Yorkshire Dales; and the wildness of the North York Moors, purple with heather in late summer.

Although it is an unofficial and mostly un-signposted trail, it attracts thousands of walkers each year. With its constantly changing scenery it also makes a superb running trip that will test your ability to navigate. Today there's even an ultra-marathon – the Northern Traverse – where runners complete the 190-mile journey in a non-stop self-supported race. But however long you take to make the trip, heed Wainwright's advice and give yourself plenty of time to 'stand and stare'.

For a 10-day itinerary, suggested overnight stops are Ennerdale Bridge, Borrowdale, Patterdale, Shap, Kirkby Stephen, Reeth, Danby Wiske, Clay Bank Top (guesthouses off-route at Great Broughton and Chop Gate) and Glaisdale.

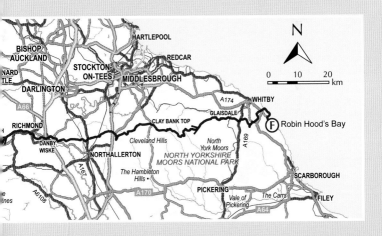

Hasty Bank in the Cleveland Hills

The route

After the rolling countryside around St Bees, high passes and valley paths lead you through Enerdale, **Borrowdale**, **Grasmere** and **Patterdale** before dropping to the shores of **Haweswater** to leave the Lake District and continue on to **Kirkby Stephen** and the Pennines. From here it's a traverse of the Yorkshire Dales through **Keld**, **Swaledale** and **Reeth**, and on to the historic town of **Richmond**. The Vale of Mowbray offers respite before the **Cleveland Hills** and

a superb crossing of the **North York Moors** before cliff-top paths lead to the finale of **Robin Hood's Bay**.

Highlights

- The satisfaction of running right across the country, from the Irish Sea to the North Sea, taking in the changes as you go
- The variety and beauty of the landscapes in three contrasting national parks

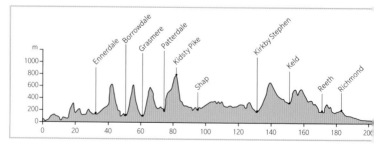

> ## Look out for...

Wainwright baggers. Over a period of 13 years, Wainwright produced seven books in his *A Pictorial Guide to the Lakeland Fells* series, featuring his favourite mountains and exquisite hand-drawn illustrations. Bagging all 214 peaks is popular with walkers, and the list provides an irresistible challenge to some hardy runners. The first to do it was Alan Heaton in 1985, who ran the 515km circuit, with 36,000m ascent, in 9 days, 16 hours and 42 minutes. The following year, the legendary fell runner Joss Naylor completed the round in 7 days and 1 hour. The record stood until 2014 and Steve Birkinshaw's time of 6 days and 13 hours, involving two marathons and over 5,000m of ascent every day.

- The interesting towns and villages visited en route
- Great running on a wide variety of terrain
- The navigational challenge of finding your own way on an iconic, yet unmarked route.

Top tips

- You can use baggage transfer services on this route
- The Coast to Coast route can be broken down into shorter trips and some baggage transfer companies offer car parking and transport

between key locations on the way, making this easier

- You need to have good mountain skills and be prepared for quickly changing weather since you will be climbing high passes in the Lakes
- Run from west to east so that the prevailing weather will be coming from behind
- The route drops through some villages and a couple of towns, but it's best to carry a day's water and food and resupply at the end of the day.

Where to find out more

- *The Coast to Coast Walk* by Terry Marsh (Cicerone Press)
- *A Coast to Coast Walk* by Alfred Wainwright (Frances Lincoln)
- The Wainwright Society website has a section on the route: www.wainwright.org.uk/coasttocoast.html
- Contour Trail Running Holidays offer this route as a supported, self-guided trip: www.contoursrun.co.uk

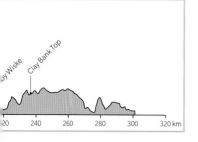

'I think that mountain there is Helvellyn,' said the walker, looking up from his map and pointing to the ridge above. He sounded American.

I was perched on a rock above Grisedale Tarn, unwrapping a chocolate bar and enjoying the lofty views from my second pass of the day. That morning I'd already run through the wild Langstrath valley and crossed the heights of Greenup Edge, before a long descent to Grasmere and a stiff climb had brought me to this point. Far below, by Ullswater, was my bed for the night in Patterdale youth hostel.

It was a warm, sunny June afternoon, with blue skies and scuttling clouds reflected in the still lake. Nearby, a couple were also having drinks and snacks, alongside the man poring over his map. Behind us, an elderly woman, possibly in her mid-70s, appeared at the col. Frail and birdlike, she was moving slowly on the path, placing her trekking poles with great concentration. It appeared she was being shepherded by another woman, walking just behind her.

'Hey Mom, that mountain is Helvellyn,' he said, addressing the new arrivals, who were now looking for a place to sit. 'Didn't we climb that 30 years ago?'

A day later, on my journey to Shap, over the highest part of the route, I was surprised to see the family again. This time they were sat resting, close to High Street (named after the ancient Roman road that once ran over its summit). They recognised me, giving a friendly, 'Hey it's the runner!'

They were walking the Coast to Coast over 15 days and averaging less than two miles an hour. The older woman's pace meant a 5am start and trekking until the last of the daylight dimmed. She had grown up in Cumbria but had moved to the States after meeting her American husband. The couples were her two children and their partners. As I left them, I thought about that young mother having brought her children to the Lakeland fells before returning a lifetime later to fulfil a long-held dream.

A tale from the trail
Coast to Coast

I, too, was fulfilling an ambition: to run Wainwright's iconic route across England. But despite the popularity of the walk, it seemed runners were a rarity, generating curiosity and amusement. 'Are you running the Coast to Coast?' was a question I was asked everywhere. In pubs and guesthouses, walkers recognised me as the woman who had passed them earlier that day. Some were visibly startled as I jogged past, and a couple of times I even heard swearing!

But the Coast to Coast is a fantastic route for trail running. I climbed Cumbrian passes high above lakes that were glistening in summer sunshine. Swathes of cotton grass whitened the fells, while sheep grazed in pastures blazing with buttercups. In the Yorkshire Dales, wind sang in my ears as I descended starkly beautiful moors to lush Swaledale and through meadows dotted with pale limestone barns. Above the valley, hidden hillsides lay scarred by the former lead mining industry. In North Yorkshire I crossed bilberry- and heather-clad moorland, where ancient stone faces and signposts loomed in morning mist. There, starting earlier than the walkers, I found myself gloriously alone with only squawking red grouse and scurrying pheasants for company.

On a cool, breezy afternoon I trotted along cliff tops toward my final destination of Robin Hood's Bay. This rugged coast, often shrouded in mist, has seen many a wrecked ship in the past. Passing dog-walkers, I dropped steeply on yellow, gorse-lined footpaths to the village with its colourful fishermen's cottages, where tourists in the narrow lanes were oblivious to my journey's end.

As tradition demanded, I wandered across the shining sand to the blue-grey sea where I tossed in the pebble I'd carried from St Bees, before dipping my feet in the water. Here, by the cold waves of the North Sea, a woman in colourful hiking gear beamed at me.

'Didn't you run past me yesterday?' she asked. 'My legs hurt just walking. Why are you running?'

I laughed and wondered how to respond. Devising the route had been a labour of love for Alfred Wainwright; he'd wanted to map out a journey over the finest ground in Northern England. Knowing this, the question really was, 'Why *wouldn't* I?'

Grizedale Tarn – up high in the Lake District

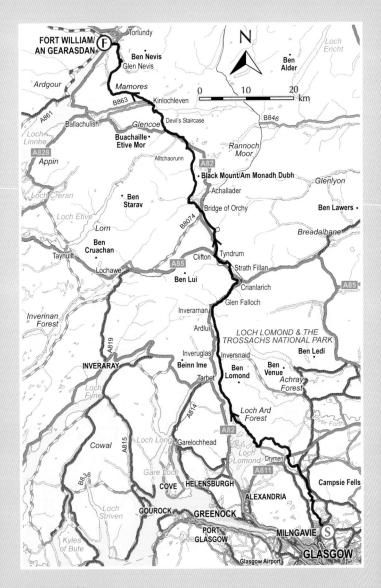

ROUTE 7
West Highland Way

Through the magnificent Highlands on Scotland's most famous trail

Start	Milngavie
Finish	Fort William
Distance	153km (95 miles)
Total ascent	4160m (13,650ft)
Duration	5 days comfortably, or 4 days of marathon-distance running
Terrain	Very runnable tracks and drovers' roads but there's a very rough, rocky section on the side of Loch Lomond and also descending the Devil's Staircase.
High point	Devil's Staircase summit, 548m (1798ft)
Navigation	Straightforward – route is well waymarked
Where to stay	Hotels, B&Bs, guesthouses, youth hostels, camping barns and campsites en route. Wild camping is not really an option.

Steeped in history, this superb national trail takes you north from Milngavie on the outskirts of Glasgow to Fort William in the shadow of Ben Nevis, Britain's highest mountain. From the rolling East Dunbartonshire countryside and the waterside trails of Loch Lomond, to the remote wilderness of Rannoch Moor and the dramatic mountains of Glencoe; the variety of landscapes along the way makes this one of Scotland's best-known long-distance walks.

The route is almost entirely off-road, following ancient drovers' roads, farm paths and old military tracks built to help in the control of Jacobite clansmen. It offers great running on excellent, well-marked trails through some of the most magnificent mountain scenery in Britain.

In 1985, Bobby Shields and Duncan Watson ran the route in 17 hours and 48 minutes. Their adventure was the beginning of an annual West Highland Way race, with a cut-off of 35 hours. Taken at a more leisurely pace, the route makes for a truly memorable fastpacking journey – one that is ideal for novices and experts alike.

Possible overnight stops for a five-day itinerary are Balmaha, Inverarnan, Bridge of Orchy and Kinlochleven.

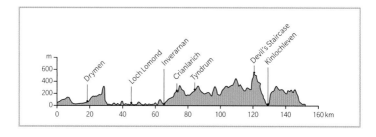

The route

The trail starts at Milngavie and passes through Mugdock Country Park and Drymen before going on to follow the shores of **Loch Lomond**, passing Ben Lomond and continuing on through **Glen Falloch** and **StrathFillan** to **Tyndrum**. From here it crosses Rannoch Moor, passing Buachaille Etive Mor to reach the head of **Glencoe**, and climbs the **Devil's Staircase** before descending to **Kinlochleven**. The final stretch goes through Lairig Mor on the southern flanks of the Mamores, before entering **Glen Nevis** and finishing at Gordon Square in **Fort William**.

Highlights

- Superb variety of scenery, from lowlands to Highlands
- Excellent running on the route of one of the UK's most iconic ultra-marathons
- Well-marked route, with good paths and tracks throughout
- The feeling of being remote, despite never being too far from civilisation
- Plentiful accommodation, services and refreshments providing opportunities for a comfortable and relaxing end to a day's running.

> ## Look out for...

Spiderman. In 2015, Ross Lawrie ran the West Highland Way race dressed as Spiderman, to raise money for the Children's Hospice Association of Scotland. He had worn the costume for previous charity events and it seemed an obvious thing to do when he became an ultra-runner. Ross had previously completed the race in less than 24 hours, and dressed as the superhero his biggest concern was whether he'd be able to see at night even using a head torch. Spiderman successfully completed the event and has since also accompanied Ross while fastpacking in the Cairngorms.

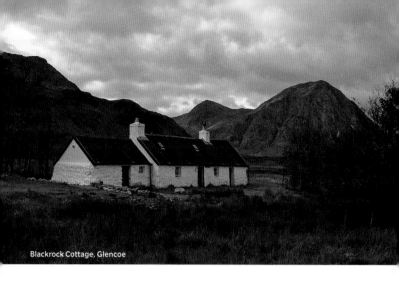

Blackrock Cottage, Glencoe

Top tips
- You can use baggage transfer services on this route
- Be prepared for quickly changing Highland weather
- Midges are a problem, primarily from June to August – carry repellent
- This is a popular hiking route, so it's advisable to book accommodation in advance, especially in summer.

Where to find out more
- *The West Highland Way* by Terry Marsh (Cicerone Press)
- West Highland Way website: www.westhighlandway.org
- Contour Trail Running Holidays offer this route as a supported, self-guided trip: www.contoursrun.co.uk

The Black Mount between Glen Orchy and Glencoe

On the loch, a few people were messing about in kayaks and a girl was preparing to go zorbing. I waded into the water up to my thighs; it was surprisingly warm for September – too warm to chill my legs. We were in Balmaha, on the shores of Loch Lomond, having run 20 miles from Milngavie, the start of the West Highland Way. I'd hoped a dip would freshen my legs for four more days of running, but I'd have to run a cold bath in the B&B instead.

Mike, the B&B owner, had heard it was my birthday the following day and kindly offered us free use of his kayaks to visit the wooded islands on the loch, some of which were inhabited by nuns in the eighth century. We politely declined the offer, wanting a rest and a lazy afternoon – only to find a bottle of red wine outside our door instead! I wasn't sure which birthday gift would have been the most detrimental

to our running, but it was a lovely gesture and made the chilly bath more bearable.

As it was, only the legs of Nicky Spinks or Jasmin Paris would have helped me the next morning. I'd assumed the shores of Loch Lomond to be easy, flat running, but this section was technical and rocky, with tree roots and big climbs and descents. I found it impossible to run. I may even have been scrambling in places! And I almost physically recoiled when we passed some German hikers with packs nearly as big as they were. How were they managing on this roller-coaster trail? Thankfully the path levelled out for some great running through autumn woodland alongside the gleaming loch which reflected blue skies and the red hawthorn and rowan of the shore.

The autumn Highlands still had a few remaining summer visitors – the Scottish midges. On the edge of forest, approaching

A tale from the trail
West Highland Way

Rannoch Moor, they clouded around us despite the slick of sweet-smelling Avon 'Skin-so-Soft' on our bare skin. I wasn't bitten, but soon my face was peppered with the tiny black insects. It was warm and rainy as we crossed the sweeping moorland with its patchwork of silvery lochans. Shrouded in cloud, the summits of the Black Mount rose above us as we passed heathered braes and crossed babbling burns that flowed over bouldery streambeds.

Beneath the White Corries we dropped into Glencoe, splashing through puddles on an ancient track as we descended to Blackrock Cottage, transfixed by the sudden appearance of Buchaille Etive Mor which dominates the glen. In Gaelic, Glencoe means 'Glen of Weeping', and the steep-sided valley had a dark, dramatic beauty in the rainy weather. Small rainbows arched across wisps of cloud in the valley-bottom while the hillsides glowed with the copper sheen of September bracken.

After warming up with bowls of soup at the Kings House Hotel, an historic drovers' inn, we tackled the Devil's Staircase – the highest point on the route. The climb wasn't actually difficult; a good zig-zag path took us to the gap, from where in fine weather we would have had our first glimpse of Ben Nevis. Dropping onto a rocky trail, which was that day more of a stream, we plunged past Blackwater Reservoir to Kinlochleven, our stop for that night.

On the last day, two friends from Perth – John and Linda – joined us. Laughing and joking, we climbed out of Kinlochleven to rejoin the military road into Lairig Mor, a concealed glen known only to walkers and estate workers. With good views to Ben Nevis there were plenty of photo stops as we traversed superb, remote hill country on the flanks of the western Mamores. We passed deserted steadings and ran deep into woodland, flying down paths carpeted in pine needles, before eventually joining a fire road to slip into Glen Nevis.

The final stretch on tarmac was a shock to our legs and took us to Nevis Bridge, the end of the West Highland Way. From her bum-bag, instead of jelly babies, Linda pulled out a silver hipflask she'd been carrying all day. Our Highland journey – and my first ever fastpacking adventure – was celebrated in local fashion, with a wee Scottish dram.

Buachaille Etive Mor, Glencoe

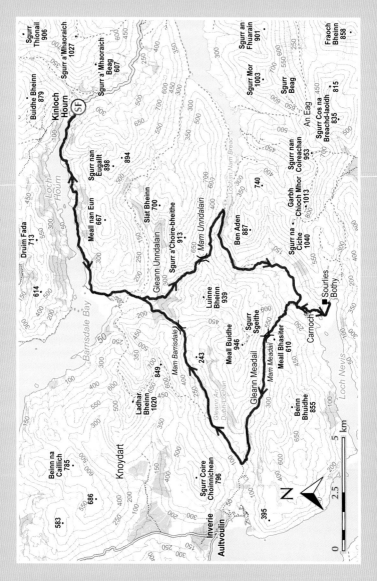

ROUTE 8
Knoydart

A two-day bothy adventure in the wilderness of the Rough Bounds

Scotland

Wales England

Start/Finish	Kinloch Hourn
Distance	60km (37 miles)
Total ascent	2620m (8,600ft)
Duration	2 days
Terrain	Good paths – although sometimes rocky, overgrown or boggy – with some faint and pathless sections. Much of the route can be run, but there are sections of muddy, rocky ground, open marsh, potentially hazardous river crossings and steep climbs and descents to contend with.
High point	Mam Unndulain and Mam Meadail are both approximately 540m (1770ft)
Navigation	Straightforward apart from some tricky route-finding near Lochan nam Breac
Where to stay	Sourlies bothy, or wild camp either at Sourlies or the ruins at Carnoch

The so-called 'Rough Bounds' of Knoydart – often described as Britain's last wilderness – are difficult to reach. Getting to the start of the route involves either a boat trip or long car journey along a winding, 20-mile single-track road. Cut off from the UK road network, the peninsula is a wild place of rugged mountains, remote glens and fjord-like sea lochs. This spectacular area includes three Munros and its coastal views take in Skye and the islands of the Inner Hebrides.

In the 19th century the peninsula fell victim to the Highland clearances, but since 1999, after huge fundraising efforts, the land has been owned and managed by its own small community. Some days you won't bump into another soul here – although you may spot minke whales, eagles, otters and stags.

Despite its inaccessibility, there are good paths connecting the glens and these provide exceptional running through challenging terrain. This fastpacking circuit is a wonderful way to immerse yourself in the unique landscape.

The route

From Kinloch Hourn the route takes an undulating path to **Barrisdale Bay** before climbing up through **Gleann Unndalain** and then dropping to **Lochan nam Breac** to follow the River Carnach out to **Loch Nevis** (fording the river twice). Cross the river at the footbridge at **Carnoch** and then, depending on the tide, either go around or over the headland to **Sourlies**. Next day it's back to **Carnoch**, then over the pass (Mam Meadail) between **Meall Bhasiter** and Sgurr Sgeithe for a fabulous descent through **Gleann Meadail** to join the Inverie-Barrisdale track. This carries you over **Mam Barrisdale** and back to **Barrisdale Bay**, from where you retrace your steps to the start.

Highlights

- A truly special wilderness experience in a remote and spectacular location
- A superb route on a legacy network of well-made paths through wild terrain
- Spectacular views of rugged mountain and coastal scenery
- Plentiful wildlife including red deer, otters, pine martens, and birds of prey such as golden eagles
- An overnight stay or wild camp at Sourlies bothy
- Excellent running, descending off the passes and along loch-side paths.

Top tips

- Be prepared for a serious run in a remote area with limited escape options. You will be a long way from help if you have an accident;

Into the wild. Descending from the pass of Mam Unndalain

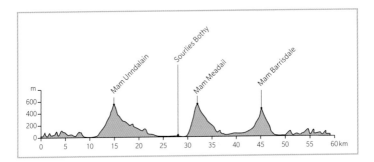

therefore you need to be self-sufficient with good wilderness skills

- The route involves crossing the River Carnach twice by fording it and a third time over the Carnoch Bridge. The river is hazardous when in spate and there is risk of death. The river crossings can be avoided by descending to the valley directly from Mam Unndalain. Further details are available in the route information sheet at the link below

- Always carry a tent in case the bothy is full or you're forced to wild camp elsewhere due to unforeseen circumstances. Sourlies and Barrisdale are popular bothies – especially in the summer and at weekends when kayak groups also use them

BE AWARE

To get to Sourlies bothy it is necessary to cross the River Carnach at Carnoch, where there is a bridge, and then go around or over the headland to the bothy. Shortly before this book went to print, Carnoch Bridge was condemned as unsafe. It can no longer be used and is in the process of being removed and replaced. Updates on the bridge replacement can be obtained from the Knoydart Foundation at their website, www.knoydart-foundation.com, or on their Facebook page.

By Carnoch Bridge, the river can be forded in dry spells in the spring and summer but, on the whole, it is impassable there. People have died trying to ford it and those who dare to attempt this need to be fully aware of the risk. If safety is in doubt due to high water levels, omit the out-and-back to Sourlies and camp at the Carnoch ruin.

- Be prepared for quickly changing weather
- This route crosses land used for deer stalking; however, you should be unaffected if you stick to the paths and avoid causing disturbance. Anyone planning to venture off footpaths should find out from the estates if stalking is taking place. Those visited on this route include Kilchoan (www.kilchoan-knoydart.com), Barrisdale (www.barrisdaleestate.com) and Camusrory (general advice for Camusrory may be available from the Knoydart Foundation via www.knoydart-foundation.com)
- If two days is too challenging, consider a three-day fastpack with overnight stays in Sourlies bothy and Inverie, before returning to Kinloch Hourn
- If necessary, the journey can be broken in either direction by staying at Barrisdale bothy or camping there. Barrisdale bothy has a toilet and tap

Weaving across the marsh to get to Sourlies bothy

Sea views from Mam Meadail
(Photo credit: Chris Councell)

- Midges can be an issue in the summer months, so carry repellent just in case.

Where to find out more
- For more on this route, see: https://www.cicerone.co.uk/957

- This is a featured route in *Scottish Trail Running* by Susie Allison (Pesda Press)
- www.knoydart-foundation.com
- www.visitknoydart.co.uk

> **Look out for...**

The white-tailed eagle. Also known as the sea eagle, this is the largest bird of prey in the UK and the fourth largest eagle in the world. Standing at a height of almost a metre, its wingspan can reach almost 2.5m.

Hunted to extinction here in the 1800s, this eagle has been successfully reintroduced to the west and east coasts of Scotland. Breeding pairs are now found on the Isle of Skye, Rum, Mull and several sites on the west coast.

Other than by its size, the white-tailed eagle is identifiable by a pale head, white, wedge-shaped tail and broad rectangular wings. The birds are scavengers but will also hunt for fish, rabbits and seabirds.

Stepping cautiously over the rickety bridge, my stomach fluttered as I glimpsed the river through the gaps in the planks. Safely across, we saw the tide was in, meaning a shoreline walk to the bothy was out of the question. We'd have to cross the marsh in fading light. As we slowly wove our way, testing the boggy ground and ponds with our poles, suddenly, all around us, the reeds and grass appeared to be on fire. A rain shower over the loch had been lit gold by the setting sun. Lasting only moments, it was one of the most beautiful things I'd ever seen.

Muddy deer tracks carried us over the steep headland, before finally dropping us to the bothy. Pushing open the door, in the half-light I saw the room was empty and the bunks bare. On the table, the bothy book lay open and someone had left behind a tin of baked beans. Fresh driftwood lay piled by the fireplace. It seemed we had the place to ourselves. Relieved to peel the packs off our backs, we set about making ourselves at home.

It was 7pm on an October evening in Sourlies bothy, at the end of the first day of our 40-mile circuit around Knoydart. That morning we'd run along Loch Hourn, on slopes of wind-twisted pines and rhododendron, to Barrisdale Bay. Here, rocky islands drew our gaze towards Skye and craggy mountains rose above the valley, red with bracken. Two golden eagles circled above, while oystercatchers cried on the shore.

From the bay we climbed stalkers' paths to Gleann Unndalain, looking up whenever we heard stags roar. Straining our eyes, we usually spotted the harem first – dark shapes moving on the hillside – and then the male, watching us from a

A tale from the trail
Knoydart

high perch. Often we saw hoof prints in the mud and a deep, musky odour would suddenly scent the air.

From the pass, we peered into a wild gorge that widened into a valley, with a river snaking south and glinting in the afternoon sun. We zig-zagged down the sodden hillside to the water, where we waded across the shallows to follow its course out to Loch Nevis. We trod the rocky, slippery trails with exquisite care – we were now a day in any direction from human habitation.

Later, in the bothy, as we lay in our sleeping bags, candlelight flickered and lit up a ram's skull and guitar hanging over the fireplace. I'd read of walkers staying here who'd cooked up mussels from the shore, but we'd concocted a three-course dinner of soup, noodles and custard, followed by chocolate and a dram of apricot brandy. As we ate, we watched a stag, just metres from the building, and it was now roaring in the darkness. It was only 8.30pm but we were exhausted and we fell asleep to that haunting bellow, along with the thundering of a nearby waterfall and the patter of mice.

The next morning we retraced our steps to Carnoch, passing deer on the marsh, before climbing to a bealach where superb sea views opened up. A fantastic descent took us to Gleann an Dubh Lochain, where we resisted the temptation to turn left for Inverie – home to The Old Forge, Britain's most remote pub. Instead we took the track loch-side to Mam Barrisdale, our second pass of the day, meeting the first and only hiker we saw throughout our trip before dropping back into Glean Barrisdale.

It was early evening as we made our way back along the final six miles of roller-coaster trail to Kinloch Hourn. In gathering dusk, with curtains of rain and mist hanging in the valley, the autumn bracken and red lichen seemed to glow. From the water, we suddenly heard a growl and hiss, accompanied by quacks and splashing. Maybe an otter trying to catch a duck supper? During the final mile, our head torches lit the rain and we waded calf-deep in water where the loch had submerged the path. Finally, the orange lights of the farmhouse appeared and we heard the hum of their generator.

Soon we were driving along a single-track road on the long journey home. However, I knew I would have to return one day – I had left my heart in the rugged wilderness of the Rough Bounds.

An October sunset lights up a rain shower over Loch Nevis (Photo credit: Chris Councell)

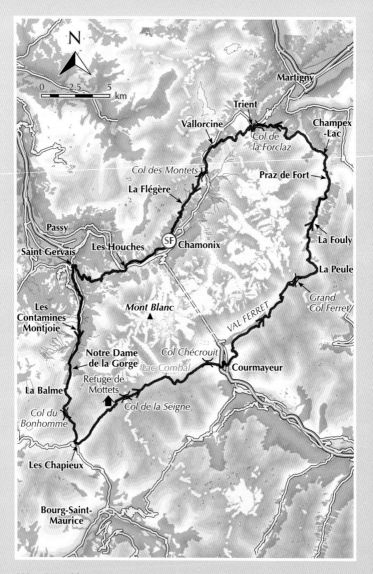

N

0   2.5   5
km

Martigny

Trient

Vallorcine

Col de la Forclaz

Champex-Lac

Col des Montets

Praz de Fort

La Flégère

La Fouly

Passy

Les Houches

SF   Chamonix

La Peule

Saint Gervais

Grand Col Ferret

VAL FERRET

Les Contamines Montjoie

Mont Blanc ▲

Notre Dame de la Gorge

Col Chécrouit

Lac Combal

Courmayeur

La Balme

Refuge de Mottets

Col de la Seigne

Col du Bonhomme

Les Chapieux

Bourg-Saint-Maurice

Europe

ROUTE 9
Ultra Trail du Mont Blanc

Hut-to-hut around Europe's highest mountain

Start/Finish	Chamonix
Distance	168km (104 miles)
Total ascent	9620m (31,560ft)
Duration	5–6 days is comfortable, or can be done in 3 or 4 days
Terrain	Good mountain and valley tracks and paths (some single-track) with some small areas of rough ground. After any climb to a col, the valley descents are generally very runnable. Short section of ladders around Aiguillette d'Argentière but this can be avoided by a variant.
High point	Grand Col Ferret, 2525m (8284ft)
Navigation	Straightforward – route is well signposted
Where to stay	Hotels, hostels, mountain huts, camping

The Tour du Mont Blanc is one of the most popular long-distance walks in Europe. It circles the Mont Blanc massif, starting in the Alpine mecca of Chamonix, France, before passing into Italy and a wild corner of Switzerland and then descending back into France.

The Ultra Trail du Mont Blanc (UTMB) is the most famous ultra-marathon in the world and basically follows the walking route. It is widely regarded as one of the most difficult races in Europe, and is one of the largest with over 2000 starters, who have 46.5 hours to complete the event. The quickest finish in less than 20 hours.

Running the circuit around Mont Blanc is a goal for thousands of runners every year – either in the event or for a personal challenge. With a total ascent of over the height of Everest, it's a mammoth undertaking in one push, but taken at a more leisurely pace it makes for a fantastic fastpacking trip.

On a six-day itinerary, overnight stops are likely to be Les Contamines, Refuge des Mottets, Courmayeur, La Fouly and Trient.

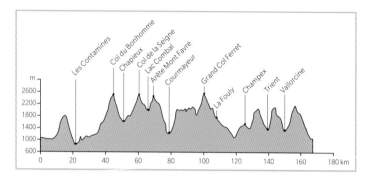

Highlights

- Hut-to-hut Alpine fastpacking
- Plentiful huts, inns and valley hotels make for easy rest and resupply
- Experience of the most iconic ultra in the world
- Superb running with long valley descents and not especially technical terrain
- The cultures of three different countries
- High-quality, well-marked trails
- Variants that can be interspersed with the main route
- Exhilarating, spectacular Alpine mountain scenery

The route

From Chamonix the route heads via **Les Houches** to **Les Contamines**, past **Notre Dame de la Gorge** and up to **Col du Bonhomme** before descending to **Les Chapieux** and **Ville des Glaciers**. From here, **Col de la Seigne** is the gateway into Italy and Val Veny leads to a climb over **Col Chécrouit** to **Courmayeur**; then the route continues via **Val Ferret** and **Grand Col Ferret** into Switzerland. It's then on through Swiss Val Ferret and **Champex** before continuing on to **Col de la Forclaz** and **Trient**. Finally you head to **Vallorcine**, **Col des Montets** and **La Flégère** before returning to **Chamonix**.

Top tips

- Leave any spare gear at your hotel
- Go light, resupplying at huts and villages. Huts serve hot meals and refreshments and the villages en route have shops
- Refill water bottles at huts and from water troughs en route
- At Aiguillette d'Argentière the way ascends metal ladders, rungs and handrails fixed on rock walls. This can be avoided by taking a variant
- In the Alps, thunderstorms are common – be aware of what you should do if you get caught in one. Advice can be found at www.mountainsafety.co.uk and the BMC website: www.thebmc.co.uk
- Be prepared for all mountain weather, including snow even in summer

Rifugio Elisabetta stands on a spur overlooking the Vallon de la Lée Blanche

- Consider using lifts, buses and taxis to shorten the route if pressed for time
- There are companies who will organise your accommodation and/or move your bags between overnight stops.

Where to find out more

- *Trail Running: Chamonix and the Mont Blanc Region* by Kingsley Jones (Cicerone Press)
- *Tour of Mont Blanc* by Kev Reynolds (Cicerone Press)
- Run the Alps offer this route as a guided and self-guided trip: runthealps.com

> ### Did you know?

One of UTMB's sister events is La Petite Trotte à Léon. Taking place in the same week, this extreme race is an enlarged 290km circuit of Mont Blanc with 24,000m of climbing and a cut-off of 136 hours. There are no course markings and the route is on technical, trackless terrain; competitors run, hike and scramble their way over passes and summits for nearly six days. They compete in small teams, self-supported, carrying food and water and using mountain refuges and villages for rest and resupply. With the exception of three checkpoints, there is no other aid. You're not given a finishing position – you either finish or you don't.

It was mid-afternoon when we reached Grand Col Ferret on the Italian-Swiss border – Tour du Mont Blanc's highest point at just over 2500m. Sitting on the grass in the sunshine, sharing cheese and chocolate we'd bought in Courmayeur, we gazed into the Alpine amphitheatre with Mont Blanc's snowy peak floating in the blue sky. Nearby was the Peuterey ridge, and beyond that the infamous Innominata. It was hard to believe that, starting from Courmayeur, the Catalonian runner Kilian Jornet had run and climbed his way over this knife-edged ridge and then Mont Blanc's summit to reach Chamonix less than nine hours later. Nicknamed 'the all-terrain human', he has also won the Ultra Tour du Mont Blanc three times, completing the route in less than 21 hours. In contrast, our run would be over a lazy six days, stopping in mountain refuges and valley hotels en route.

On the morning of our fourth day on the trail we'd enjoyed flowing single-track high above Val Ferret, looking onto the flanks of the mountain with its savage rock walls, ridges and tumbling glaciers. The path had contoured above terraced fields and farms, on hillsides red with September bilberry and rowan. Stopping to fill our bottles at Rifugio Bonatti, the spring water had been cold and sweet. Four visitors were sitting at the terrace, talking and laughing, enjoying plates of food and a bottle of wine. The delicious smell of grilled cheese made had our mouths water, but we'd pressed on.

From Grand Col Ferret it was a fast, fun descent on sweeping trails into the next valley. Although still beautiful, the Swiss Val Ferret was more bucolic and peaceful, lacking the drama of the earlier views. We dropped through a succession of lush pastures, passing tiny villages and hamlets of timber and stone buildings. The quiet was broken only by cowbells, which intensified on reaching a dairy farm where a large herd was being led home for afternoon milking. In La Fouly that evening, as a vegetarian and not wanting yet another omelette, I was served a plate piled high with slabs of local cheese. I couldn't really stomach it so close to bedtime, but with the next morning's fresh bread that was lunch sorted!

The Tour du Mont Blanc is the most popular mountain walk in Europe and on our circuit we met people from all over the

A tale from the trail
Ultra Trail du Mont Blanc

ROUTE 10
Dolomites Alta Via 1

On the 'high ways' through the Pale Mountains

Start	Lago di Braies
Finish	Listolade
Distance	84km (52 miles)
Total ascent	4500m (14,760ft)
Duration	4½ days
Terrain	Generally good paths with occasional exposed sections. From Forcella del Lago the route descends a very steep gulley on a timber-reinforced path. Overall a very runnable route, apart from around the passes, some big climbs and some traverses on loose scree.
High point	Forcella Lagazuoi 2573m (8442ft)
Navigation	Although the route is generally waymarked, map-reading skills are required.
Where to stay	Mountain refuges, valley hotels

The Dolomites are a UNESCO World Heritage Site with some of the most beautiful and distinctive limestone mountain landscapes in the world, comprising vertical walls, sheer cliffs, steeples, pinnacles and deep, long valleys. Well-marked hiking routes snake through the range, supported by a network of characterful *rifugi* or mountain huts. The area also boasts deciduous and evergreen forests, fascinating wildlife and beautiful Alpine meadows.

Known also as the 'Pale Mountains', the region is home to several *Alta Via* routes – meaning 'High Route' or 'High Way' in Italian. Alta Via 1 is the classic trail in the Dolomites and also the easiest, stretching 118km from Lago di Braies in the north to La Pissa in the south. The fastpacking route described here is a truncated version of Alta Via 1 and uses variants to largely avoid aided and exposed sections, providing superb running through magnificent surroundings.

Overnight stops are at Rifugio Fanes, Rifugio Scoiattoli, Rifugio Coldai and Rifugio Vazzoler. The route could also be done in four days by skipping the stay at Rifugio Vazzoler and continuing directly to Listolade.

The route

From Lago di Braies the route climbs and crosses a plateau to reach **Rifugio Biella**, and then drops before climbing again to **Rifugio Fanes**. Next it's up to **Forcella del Lago**, into the Cortina Dolomites, where a steep descent precedes a long pull up to **Rifugio Lagazuoi**. There's a short easterly section before the route drops to the Cortina–Passo Falzarego road, from where it's up to **Cinque Torri** and **Rifugio Scoiattoli** before taking a route variant to **Passo Giau** and an open pasture basin, and on to **Passo Staulanza**. A traverse of the Pelmo region is followed by a climb to **Rifugio Coldai**, then the route goes through the Civetta to **Rifugio Vazzoler**. Here you leave the main AV1 route for an easy descent to **Listolade** where you can connect with major towns.

Highlights

- Breathtaking scenery on a route that gives the feeling of being intimate and up close with the mountains
- Frequent (and excellent) mountain huts where you can enjoy Italian hospitality and food
- Travelling fast and light on a hut-to-hut journey
- Good public transport, making the route both accessible and flexible
- A lot of runnable trails, apart from around the passes, some big climbs and some traverses on scree

- Plentiful wildlife, and Alpine meadows that are transformed in summer into seas of wildflowers.

Top tips

- Consider leaving spare gear at the airport, railway station left luggage or at a hotel, depending on your travel plans
- The abundance of mountain huts means you can eat and resupply at these, rather than carrying everything
- It's advisable to pre-book accommodation in summer as this route is popular with organised groups
- Camping is forbidden along the route
- Afternoon thunderstorms are common – be aware of what you should do if you get caught in one. Advice can be found at www.mountainsafety.co.uk and the BMC website: www.thebmc.co.uk
- Be prepared for all mountain weather, including snow even in summer

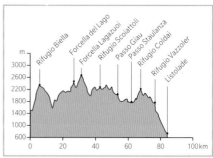

Morning mist on the way to Passo di Limo (Photo credit: Chris Councell)

Where to find out more

- *Trekking in the Dolomites: Alta Via 1 and Alta Via 2* by Gillian Price (Cicerone Press)

- Holimites offer this and other routes in the Dolomites as escorted and self-guided trail-running holidays: www.holimites.com

> ### Look out for...

People on the via ferrata, or 'iron paths' in Italian. This is an extraordinary mix of Alpine trekking and protected rock climbing, using cables and a harness. Its origins are most often associated with the First World War (although they were developed prior to this) when several were erected in the Dolomites – the front line between the Italian and Austro-Hungarian troops – to help troops move at high altitude in difficult conditions. Today, steel cables have replaced ropes; metal ladders and rungs have taken the place of flimsy wooden structures; and people from far and wide visit the region for this unique style of mountaineering.

Outside, the evening sky was suddenly filled with a blinding white flash which illuminated the outline of the Cinque Torri, the five limestone towers opposite our mountain hut at 2300m. Then everything returned to purple-blackness and rain lashed the windowpanes as a deafening clap of thunder echoed through the valley. Far below us, village lights twinkled in the darkness.

We were sitting in the wood-panelled dining room of Rifugio Scoiattoli, waiting for dinner and poring over maps. The heavy door of the hut swung open and four walkers came in, head-to-toe in glistening waterproofs, dripping onto the floor as they peeled back hoods and discarded sodden backpacks. We were lucky to have missed being caught in the storm that afternoon.

Suddenly, the sky flared with sheet lightning and the lights in the room went out. Everyone gasped.

'Wow – did we bring our head torches down to dinner?' I laughed nervously.

Moments later the kitchen sprang back into life, accompanied by the throb of a generator. Within minutes, the diminutive, pretty Italian hut owner was lighting candles at the dining tables, while her husband resumed cooking.

Miraculously, they served us a three-course meal while the storm raged outside. By candlelight we feasted on pasta, wild mushrooms, grilled vegetables, polenta, and berry tart for dessert. As we ate, we chatted to the three men at the next table – Belgian brothers in their 60s who came each year to climb in the Dolomites, where their Italian father had grown up.

Introducing us to pine and cumin grappa – an acquired taste – they told of how their father, an Italian translator and prisoner of war, had fallen in love with their mother, a German nurse, when he was translating for Italian soldiers in the prison camp. Against her family's wishes, they later married and moved to his family's farm in a remote Dolomite valley. They eventually settled in Belgium, where the brothers grew up, but all had retained a deep love for and connection with their Italian roots and the mountains. We shared stories until late, then left them to their potent drink and trod carefully through dark corridors to our pitch-black dormitory and the deep sleep of happy runners.

A tale from the trail
Dolomites
Alta Via 1

It was the end of our second of four days fastpacking in the Dolomites, on the Alta Via 1 route. That morning, we'd left the sprawling Rifugio Fanes to run through landscapes of silvery-grey steeples and pinnacles, where we'd half expected dinosaurs to appear. We'd climbed to a notch between two towering peaks, the pass of Forcella del Lago, where through mist we'd heard the rumble of falling rock, leading our gaze up to a group of chamois goats perched high on the scree. From there, the descent was in a stomach-dropping gully to the jade-coloured Lago di Lagazuoi, and we were thankful for a wildly zig-zagging path, reinforced with sweet-scented pine timbers, clinging to the slopes. It was then an unending climb through Martian terrain to Rifugio Lagazuoi, where it's possible to explore deep mountain tunnels used by soldiers in the First World War.

After a bowl of soup at the rifugio we'd enjoyed a flowing descent to the valley bottom, where we surprised a marmot on a rocky outcrop, its piercing whistle warning other marmots of our approach. As we climbed through woodland that was dripping with afternoon rain, we heard birdsong and woodpeckers and saw a profusion of beautiful Alpine flowers path-side. Red-pink alpenrose made the hillsides blush; deep blue trumpet gentians burst from the grass; and we hunted for elusive milky-white edelweiss.

For four days we were immersed in the mountains, beneath sheer faces shrouded in cloud, where climbers worship and sometimes perish. Eventually we dropped into a valley for a train back to Venice, where we recovered a bag of clean clothes in order to end our trip with a day's sightseeing. On our last night we ate on the waterfront as the QE3 cruise-liner sailed by, her portholes lit like fairy lights. It seemed surreal that only a few nights earlier we'd crept into a chilly dormitory populated with snoring climbers and grappa fumes – but if you love trail running and all things Italian, then fastpacking in the Dolomites is *la dolce vita*.

Looking back on the route across the magnificent Pelmo (Photo credit: Chris Councell)

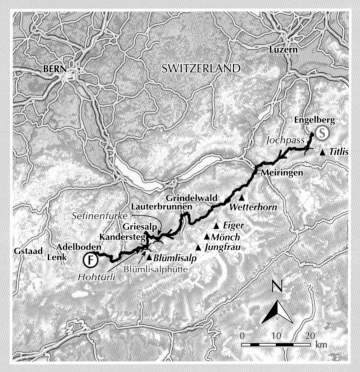

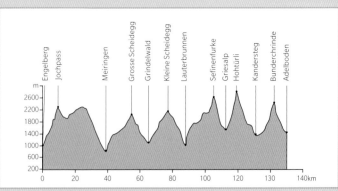

ROUTE 11
Alpine Pass Route

From east to west across Switzerland

Start	Engelberg
Finish	Adelboden
Distance	135km (84 miles)
Total ascent	8980m (29,460ft)
Duration	6 days
Terrain	Good paths, with some rocky, steep ground and steep scree slopes. Aided sections (steps, ladders, metal cables, handrails) on some passes. Some stages cross open, unforgiving terrain without easy escape routes. This is a challenging route with a lot of daily height gain, calling for self-reliance especially in wet weather and bad visibility. The valley descents are generally runnable, but there will be a lot of steep walking up to the passes.
High point	Hohtürli Pass 2778m (9114ft) (optional Blümlisalphütte, 2837m (9308ft))
Navigation	Easy – excellent waymarking throughout
Where to stay	Valley hostels and hotels (some have hikers' dormitories or massenlager), mountain huts

The Alpine Pass Route – now fully waymarked as Swiss Via Alpina 1 – is a walking route of over 350km through Switzerland, crossing high passes through the eastern Alps, Bernese Oberland and the Vaudoise and finishing at Montreux on Lake Geneva.

The Swiss VA1 route actually starts in Liechtenstein before dropping to Sargans, the traditional start of the APR. While the full route takes 2–3 weeks to walk, this fastpacking trip takes in arguably the most spectacular central stages and the highest section through the Bernese Oberland in a week. With dramatic passes, wild mountain landscapes including the Eiger, Jungfrau and Mönch, Alpine pastures and glacial lakes, this is an unforgettable journey easily ranking alongside the Tour de Mont Blanc as a classic Alpine route.

If following a 6-day itinerary, good overnight stops are: Meiringen, Grindelwald, Lauterbrunnen, Griesalp and Kandersteg. Some of these days are long and this itinerary can be extended if necessary to make the days more manageable, or some days shortened using cable cars.

Lush pastures on the way to Kleine Scheidegg
(Photo credit: Chris Councell)

The route

Out of Engelberg, the route goes over the **Jochpass** before descending to **Meiringen**. This is followed by a climb to Grosse Scheidegg and a descent to **Grindelwald**. From here you cross Kleine Scheidegg – passing the iconic Eiger, Mönch and Jungfrau – and go down into **Lauterbrunnen**, then climb past Mürren and across the **Sefinenfurke** to **Griesalp**. After crossing the **Hohtürli**, the highest col, continue onto **Kandersteg** and finally the Bunderchrinde and down to **Adelboden**.

Highlights

- Impressive Alpine scenery including iconic peaks, dramatic glaciers and lush Alpine valleys
- High passes such as the Hohtürli and Sefinenfurke
- Challenging climbs to cols followed by long valley descents that are generally runnable once you're beyond any technical terrain around the pass

- Excellent waymarking and easy navigation
- Variants providing flexibility in the route
- Excellent public transport access.

Top tips

- Water can be refilled at huts and springs en route
- Use public transport to shorten days or in case of poor weather. In bad weather, experience is needed to judge whether to cross the passes or to go around by train and bus
- Sections of climbing can be cut out using cable cars, without detracting from the experience
- Many of the descents into villages finish on steep tarmac or hard-packed trails, which is tiring on the quads
- Choose shoes with good grip on wet rock, timber and loose scree
- Some of the passes involve ladders and steps, where care must be taken as a fall here could have serious consequences

- The hardest parts of the route are around the Sefinenfurke and the Hohtürli. Both have ascents and descents over loose shale and scree. The wooden ladders (down from the Sefinenfurke and up to the Hohtürli) give solid walking but the angles are at times daunting and require a good head for heights
- Afternoon thunderstorms are common – be aware of what you should do if you get caught in one. Advice can be found at www.mountainsafety.co.uk and the BMC website: www.thebmc.co.uk
- Be prepared for all mountain weather, including snow even in summer.

Where to find out more

- *The Swiss Alpine Pass Route – Via Alpina Route 1* by Kev Reynolds (Cicerone Press)
- www.via-alpina.org

Taking care on steps on the descent from the Sefinenfurke pass

'Would you like to try our marmot and herb ointment?' grinned the hut owner at Oberi Bundalp, handing me a leaflet before serving my coffee. 'Homemade. Good for legs!'

I read the ingredients: marmot, chamois and badger fat with 13 Alpine herbs – warming for soothing muscles. I looked at the climb ahead – 1000m to the Hohtürli pass, a nick in the mountains that looked deceptively close – then back down at the cute, furry marmot on the page. I hoped a mid-morning coffee would be a sufficient boost for the next three hours of climbing.

The couple on the next table bought some local cheese 'to take our picnic at the top!' They sounded American; she was wearing a 'skort' and they were both carrying relatively small packs and wearing running shoes. Two days earlier, a British walker had asked myself and my companion if we were the US couple doing the APR – perhaps mistaking us for these two.

From the hut we crossed pasture to begin the ascent on a steep spur of dark scree and shale. It was September and unseasonably hot. On the entire six-day trip there was just one day of rain, when we'd climbed to Grosse Scheidigg, past the roaring Reichenbach falls – where Sherlock Holmes faked his death – and alongside the muddy torrent of the Reichenbach stream. I'd been cold that morning, needing soup at the pass before warming up on the flowing descent to Grindelwald.

Today, climbing in sunshine, we played tag with the Americans as we stopped for photos and to catch our breath. Cowbells rang in our ears along with the occasional marmot's whistle. Caramel-coloured cows were grazing high – one sat on the path, steadfastly refusing to move. We overtook another couple – the man carrying their toddler on his back. As if that wasn't hard enough, I noticed their son was playing with two big pebbles as his father laboured up the mountainside.

The gradient eased and a traverse led to a long flight of steps and ladders up the final slope to the pass. These weren't technical but they were steep. Not having a great head for heights, I focused on each step, placing one foot in front of the other without looking up or down.

A tale from the trail
Alpine Pass Route

Then, suddenly, we'd arrived at the Hohtürli pass, the highest point of the APR at nearly 2800m. Three hours of lung-busting, leg-burning climb were instantly forgotten as the views revealed one of the wildest, most untamed mountain landscapes I'd ever seen. The glistening Blümlisalp Massif towered above us, glaciers suspended from its slopes and wisps of cloud drifting into blue from its summit. Below us, the Kandersteg valley seemed a distant shadow below endless ridges and peaks stretching to the horizon. I could just make out the path threading through a jumble of moraines, scree and ridges below the pass, disappearing into the valley.

The Blümlisalphütte sat just above us and we climbed its steep path, decorated with cairns like a sculpture garden, to join hikers in dazzling sunshine on the terrace outside. I imagined the sunset here and was envious of those staying the night. Soon the family arrived and their toddler was happily running around while his mother unpacked a picnic and a nappy change.

After a sandwich and countless photos we dragged ourselves away. The trail dropped through screes then along moraine spurs beside icefalls. As we trotted beneath the mouths of the grey-blue glaciers, a loud bang suddenly echoed about the peaks and stopped us in our tracks – was it an avalanche?

We descended into a grassy basin, looking down onto the turquoise Oeschinen Lake which sat in a deep fjord-like trough. As we admired the view, the Americans ran past us – they were fastpacking too! Undulating forest trails led us along the lakeshore, opposite waterfalls tumbling down sheer rock. Finally, a steep trail took us to Kandersteg where we had a room booked in a local hikers' dorm.

My quads took a battering on the descent into the village, so that evening before dinner I doused my complaining thighs under a cold, then hot shower, as is my routine on multi-day runs. Despite the APR being one of the hardest (and most spectacular) fastpacking trips I've ever done, I can promise that no marmots were harmed along the way.

Three hours of climbing instantly forgotten enjoying spectacular views from the Hohtürli pass (Photo credit: Chris Councell)

Asia

ROUTE 12
Manaslu Mountain Trail Race

Running on the roof of the world

Start	Sotikhola
Finish	Dharapani
Distance	169km (105 miles)
Total ascent	10,970m (35,990ft)
Duration	12 days in total: 7 race days, 2 hiking days, 2 travelling days and 1 day briefing in Kathmandu
Terrain	Rocky, well-used trails at high altitude. In trekking season, trails are likely to be dry. Trails are runnable, but in places there will be a lot of walking due to very steep climbs, rocky terrain and altitude. At high altitudes you may encounter snow and ice.
High point	Larkya La pass, 5160m (16,929ft)
Navigation	The race is fully waymarked and has checkpoints
Where to stay	Tea houses (trekking lodges) – all accommodation is organised by the event team

The Manaslu Circuit is one of the classic tea-house treks in Nepal and considered by many to be one of the best in the Himalaya. Encircling the world's eighth highest mountain, the route is relatively undeveloped and, with far fewer trekkers, it is a much more authentic and less frequented route than its neighbour, Annapurna – providing visitors with memories of a lost Nepal.

Largely following a shortened version of the trekking route, the Manaslu Trail Race is a challenging stage race through the spectacular landscapes around the mountain. It takes runners from subtropical Hindu villages and paddy fields to Buddhist settlements high in the mountains, passing rarely visited monasteries, to the Tibetan border before crossing the pass of Larkya La. The event donates part of its proceeds to hydroelectric projects and helps distribute solar lights to the local villages.

While the route can be fastpacked independently, the requirements for a guide and permits, plus the challenges of altitude make a stage race a great option for a running expedition in the region.

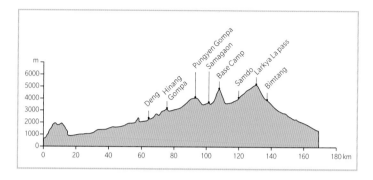

The route

From Sotikhola the route follows the Budi Gandaki river, passing **Jagat** and continuing onto **Deng**, **Bihi**, **Ghap** and **Namrung**. From here there's a diversion up a side valley for a stay at **Hinang Gompa monastery** before returning to the trail and continuing to **Sho**, **Lho** and Syala before a climb to **Pungyen** **Gompa** and a descent to **Samagaon**. From here there's a vertical kilometre race to **Manaslu Base Camp**, then the following day it's on to **Samdo** for acclimatisation and a trek to the Tibetan border before the big push over the **Larkya La pass** to **Bimtang**. The final day is almost pure descent to the finish at **Dharapani**.

Departing from Bimtang at the beginning of Stage 7
(Photo credit: © Manaslutrailrace.org Photographer Richard Bull)

Tackling the vertical kilometre race from Samagaon to Manaslu Base Camp and back (Photo credit: © Manaslutrailrace.org Photographer Richard Bull)

Highlights

- Superb trail running in a geographically spectacular region
- A variety of Himalayan landscapes, from lush subtropical valleys to sky-high peaks, lakes and glaciers
- Culturally fascinating, with Hindu and Tibetan Buddhist villages
- The wild Larkya La pass at 5160m
- Staying at a Buddhist monastery
- Peering over the border into wild Tibet
- A vertical kilometre race to Manaslu Base Camp
- The race is fully supported and gear is moved by mules and porters, so you can run with just a day-pack.

Top tips

- Running poles are essential. Take micro-spikes for crossing the pass (although these are only needed in a snowy year – the pass is usually dry during the stage race)
- Hand hygiene is crucial to staying healthy. Wash your hands regularly and use antibacterial gel
- Be aware of the risk of Acute Mountain Sickness (AMS) which is present at high altitudes and can be fatal. Further information can be found at the BMC website: www.thebmc.co.uk
- Water needs to be treated and this is taken care of by the event team
- Carry warm gear while running. As soon as sunlight leaves a valley, even as early as 2pm, it can be bitterly cold
- Be prepared for basic conditions – Asian drop toilets, few hot showers,

irregular electricity, plus no mobile phone coverage
- While there is a doctor on the trip, you need to be self-sufficient. Bring everything you might need
- Women should be aware that menstrual cycles may be affected by extreme exertion at high altitude. Bring sanitary supplies in case your cycle changes
- It's simplest to run the route as part of the event, but you can organise it independently. It's compulsory to hire a guide and obtain permits and these can be arranged through an agent or by trailrunningnepal.org

Where to find out more
- manaslutrailrace.org
- manaslucircuittrek.com
- trailrunningnepal.org
- *Trekking in the Himalaya* edited by Kev Reynolds (Cicerone Press)
- *A Trekking Guide to Manaslu and Tsum Valley* by Sian Pritchard-Jones and Bob Gibbons (Himalayan Travel Guides)
- Himalayan Adventure Labs organise guided, self-supported fastpacking trips in Nepal, specialising in the Annapurna and Langtang regions: www.himalayanadventurelabs.com

Forested, riverside trails on the long descent from Bimtang to Dharapani (Photo credit: © Manaslutrailrace.org Photographer Richard Bull)

A tale from the trail
Manaslu
Mountain Trail Race

As a teenager I was terrible at tennis, lazy in a leotard and hopeless on the hockey pitch. If you'd told me then that one day I'd race elite athletes around the world's eighth highest mountain, I would have snorted with laughter. But in November 2013, alongside Anna Frost and Lizzy Hawker, I was one of 40 runners at the start line of the Manaslu Mountain Trail, in the Nepali village of Arughat Bazaar, which was at that time the race start point. Here, a local priest anointed our foreheads with red 'tikas' before setting us on our way. This was my first stage race and my goal was to 'complete' rather than 'compete'. I'd simply entered to go trail running in a country I had long wished to see.

In Deng, on our second night, we squeezed around wooden tables, cocooned in down jackets and beanies, eating dhal and roti. Outside, in the darkness, I saw the head torch of the final runner from that day's 40km leg. As usual, I'd been one of the slowest, running the final miles alone through a shadowy, wooded gorge, abandoned by the sun as alpenglow brushed the mountaintops pink. Beneath moonlight and guided by the sound of the river, I ran towards the glow of the tiny hamlet, where the fastest runners had finished hours earlier.

That evening there was a long wait for our bags as the mules took longer than expected to arrive. Eventually I retired to a simple, bare room, and, fully dressed inside my sleeping bag, slept fitfully as temperatures plunged to minus ten. Life was hard here – even a couple of years before the region was stricken by the 2015 earthquakes. In many villages there were no schools, medical facilities or clean water, and firewood and yak dung were

still collected daily. We didn't wash for days, apart from wet-wipes or by buying a thermos of hot water. Most lodges had no electricity, while Asian squat toilets and sometimes frozen water added to our challenges.

And yet these were small things to endure in exchange for our journey around Manaslu – the 'Mountain of the Spirit'. Rivers roared below as airy trails carried us above ravines; through Hindu settlements; and past emerald rice terraces. As we climbed, the valleys opened up to reveal a wild, ethereal landscape where prayer flags laced the acres of blue above. Silvery mani-walls carved with ancient scriptures marked the entrance to Buddhist villages. Here, children played outside, bundled in thick layers against the cold.

Climbing through enchanted forest led us to the monastery and 'Shangri-La' village of Hinang Gompa, where, between shimmering peaks, the blur of a billion stars arching across a frozen black sky is forever etched in my mind. On my longest day – 13 hours – we started at 4am on moonlit paths and slowly the sunrise gilded the surrounding summits. It was a tough, slow hike to the snow-blanketed Larkya La pass at 5160m. Here, we gazed on iconic mountains in the Annapurna range before a long descent in dusk and darkness took us to the twinkling lights of Bimtang.

Above all, memories of the people stay with me: the kids running alongside us, shouting 'Namaste!' as they went to school; women laughing as they worked in barley fields on a high plateau; the couple in Samdo who shared their dung-heated hearth with curious runners, in a gloomy dwelling warmed by the yaks kept beneath; and the kind porter-cook who carried my pack when I was breathless with altitude, later guiding me down icy slopes to safety at the next village.

On the final stage to Dharapani we dropped over 2000m on forest trails, feeling the warmth on our skin and the sweet air thickening. I watched clouds floating in the valley above a thundering river, not wanting my journey to end.

Afterwards, Lizzy said, 'Perhaps each of us, in very different ways, was taken out of our comfort zone. It's then we realise our limits aren't where we thought they were, even in our day-to-day – so hold onto those dreams!'

It had been my dream to go running in the Himalaya, but my journey around Manaslu was to change my life in ways I had never dreamed possible.

The descent from Larkya La pass was slow and difficult for mules, porters and trail-runners (Photo credit: © Manaslutrailrace.org Photographer Richard Bull)

APPENDIX A
Further information and reading

Blogs on fastpacking

Excellent guide to self-sufficient fast-packing, from a US perspective
www.irunfar.com – search 'definitive guide to fastpacking'

Excellent blog on self-sufficient fast-packing by UK enthusiast 'Fastpacking Guy' www.fastpackingguy.com

Useful websites

UK ultra-distance challenges
www.gofar.org.uk

Utra-marathon and trail running news
www.irunfar.com

UK Trail Running Association
www.tra-uk.org

International Trail Running Association
www.i-tra.org

Fell Runners Association
www.fellrunner.org.uk

Welsh Fell Runners Association
www.wfra.me.uk

Scottish Hill Runners
www.scottishhillrunners.uk

Northern Ireland Mountain Running Association
www.nimra.org.uk

Irish Mountain Running Association
www.imra.ie

British Mountaineering Council
www.thebmc.co.uk

Austrian Alpine Club
(Österreichischer Alpenverein)
www.alpenverein.at

French Alpine Club (Club Alpin Français)
www.ffcam.fr

German Alpine Club
(Deutscher Alpenverein)
www.alpenverein.de

Italian Alpine Club
(Club Alpino Italiano)
www.cai.it

Swiss Alpine Club
(Schweizer Alpen-Club)
www.sac-cas.ch

Further reading

Fitness and training
Relentless Forward Progress by Bryon Powell (Breakaway, 2011)

Where the Road Ends: A Guide to Trail Running by Meghan M Hicks & Bryon Powell (Human Kinetics, 2016)

Planning your adventure
Microadventures by Alastair Humphreys (William Collins, 2014)

Grand Adventures by Alastair Humphreys (William Collins, 2016)

Wilderness Weekends by Phoebe Smith (Bradt, 2015)

Navigation and safety
Navigation for Off-Road Runners by Stuart Ferguson & Keven Shevels (Trailguides, 2007)

Downhill Techniques for Off-Road Runners by Keven Shevels (Trailguides, 2005)

Uphill Techniques for Off-Road Runners by Keven Shevels (Trailguides, 2006)

Pocket First Aid and Wilderness Medicine by Jim Duff & Ross Anderson (Cicerone, 2017)

Navigation by Pete Hawkins (Cicerone, 2017)

Advice on safety in the mountains
www.mountainsafety.co.uk

Gear and equipment
Lightweight Camping by John Traynor (Cicerone, 2017)

Further inspiration

General
The Old Ways by Robert MacFarlane (Penguin, 2013)

Runner by Lizzy Hawker (Aurum, 2015)

Feet in the Clouds by Richard Askwith (Aurum, 2004)

Wild Trails to Far Horizons by Mike Cudahy (Hayloft, 2009)

Running High by Hugh Symonds (Hayloft, 1991)

Beyond Impossible by Mimi Anderson (Summersdale, 2017)

Eat & Run by Scott Jurek (Bloomsbury, 2012)

The Art of Pilgrimage by Phil Cousineau (Conari, 2012)

The National Trails by Paddy Dillon (Cicerone, 2015)

Wales
The Welsh Three Thousand Foot Challenges by Roy Clayton & Ronald Turnbull (Grey Stone, 1997)

England
Coast to Coast by Matt Beardshall (Arima, 2007)

There is No Map In Hell by Steve Birkinshaw (Vertebrate, 2017)

Scotland
Across Scotland On Foot by Ronald Turnbull (Grey Stone, 1994)

Ireland
Mud, Sweat and Tears by Moire O'Sullivan (Moire O'Sullivan, 2011)

Overseas
Great Himalaya Trail by Gerda Pauler (Baton Wicks, 2013)

Just a Little Run Around the World by Rosie Swale Pope (Harper Collins, 2009)

Adventureman by Jamie McDonald (Summersdale, 2017)

Born to Run by Christopher McDougall (Profile, 2010)

APPENDIX B
Gear list

Essentials
- Rucksack
- Water bottle(s)
- Running shoes
- 1 long-sleeved top
- 1 short-sleeved top
- 1 shorts/capri
- 1 running tights
- 1 fleece top
- 1 windproof jacket
- 1 down or synthetic insulating 'puffer' jacket
- 1 waterproof trousers with taped seams
- 1 waterproof jacket with hood and taped seams
- 1 warm hat or beanie
- 1 pair gloves
- 1 Buff
- 1 pair running socks
- 1 sports bra
- 2 pairs underwear
- Map
- Compass
- Minimal first aid kit with blister plasters
- Survival blanket
- Head torch
- Whistle
- Mobile phone and charger
- Toothbrush and mini-toothpaste
- Mini-tube of sunscreen
- Silk sleeping bag liner (if staying in mountain huts)
- Lightweight travel towel
- Waterproof stuffsacks or large Ziploc bags

- Cash and credit cards
- Sunglasses
- Mini-tube lip balm
- Anti-chafe cream – small amount in mini Ziploc bag
- Spare empty Ziploc bag (for food)
- Pen
- 400 calories of emergency food – e.g. two Mars bars, gels

Additional gear for camping
- Tent
- Camping mat
- Sleeping bag
- Camping stove and fuel
- Matches
- Collapsible cup
- Spork
- Collapsible water carrier
- Water purification tablets
- Spare Ziploc bags for carrying out sanitary items
- Toilet paper
- Hand sanitiser

Other items to consider
- Waterproof pack cover
- Running poles
- Cap or sun-visor
- 1 spare t-shirt/top
- 1 pair waterproof gloves
- 1 pair waterproof socks
- 1 spare pair running socks
- 1 spare sports bra
- 1 pair sweat-bands
- 1 pair arm warmers

- 1 pair flip-flops or lightweight canvas shoes
- Tweezers
- Small nail clippers
- Mini sewing repair kit
- Duct tape (small amount wrapped around a chapstick)
- Mini-tube of aftersun lotion
- Energy drink powder
- Electrolyte tabs
- Tape for feet

Weight-saving tips

- If travelling with someone else, share toiletries, first aid kit and split any camping equipment between you
- Decant creams and toothpaste into mini Ziploc bags
- Cut the end off your toothbrush
- Photocopy your map onto paper
- Photocopy the relevant pages of your guidebook onto double-sided paper
- Carry copies of travel documents electronically on your phone.

Mam Barrisdale pass, on foot to the bunkhouse in Inverie, Knoydart, Scotland (Alternative route, Route 8)